HOW TO MAKE BIG MONEY ON TV

Accessing the Home Shopping Explosion Behind the Screens

Craig Daugard

UPSTART PUBLISHING
Specializing in Small Business Publishing
a division of Dearborn Publishing Group, Inc.

Executive Editor: Bobbye Middendorf
Managing Editor: Jack Kiburz
Interior Design: Lucy Jenkins
Cover Design: Design Alliance, Inc.

Published by Upstart Publishing Company,
a division of Dearborn Publishing Group, Inc.

Printed in the United States of America

96 97 98 10 9 8 7 6 5 4 3 2 1

Library of Congress Cataloging-in-Publication Data

Daugard, Craig
How to make big money on TV : accessing the home shopping explosion behind the screens / by Craig Daugard
p. cm.
Includes index.
ISBN 0-936894-99-7 (pbk.)
1. Telemarketing. 2. Teleshopping. 3. Cable television advertising. 4. Direct selling. I. Title.
HF5415.1265.D37 1995
658.8'4—dc20 95-23648
CIP

Dedication

This book is dedicated to Mari—you have a locked space in my Mind Map forever; and to my kids Jamie, Jenny and Josh Daugard—without your spending, this book would not have been necessary.

Acknowledgments

In grateful acknowledgment to Les Shekkel, Esq., for his legal advice, Tershia d'Elgin for her humor, Julie Castiglia for her persistence, my father Emmert C. Daugard, Sr., for everything he gave me, my mom Geneva Bruns for those times at the kitchen table having coffee, Emmert C. Daugard, Jr., for his money and advice, Duezzeldorf Ford for always being happy, Missy Ford because she is always antsy and my other family and friends for all their support and help. Last, but certainly not least, to my editor Bobbye Middendorf for her help, but especially her empathy.

Contents

Preface

Turning Brainstorms into Dollars

Unfortunately, many of the most novel, useful products conceived never even leave the closets of the people who dreamed them up. Why? Because these highly creative people have had no way to bring their products to market. Until now.

With the advent of home shopping channels and the Internet, however, inventors and small business people can make the big time easily and with very little investment. If you are such a person, you can put your product in front of millions of potential buyers for little or no investment, saving thousands of dollars in marketing and packaging costs. Plus, you can improve or invent new products more easily than you ever imagined. This book shows how.

How To Make Big Money on TV directs entrepreneurs onto the information superhighway. With just the seed of an idea, a person or business can use the home shopping system to first test the market, then capitalize from free advertising and wide exposure. Airing a product on television from coast to coast, even a one-person operation can compete with large conglomerates like Kodak and Mercedes-Benz.

Based on the entrepreneur's presentation to them, home shopping channels purchase a certain quantity of product. Because the lead time can be anywhere from several weeks to several months, the businessperson has time to manufacture and ship the amount ordered. The sale is ensured. There is no marketing, no sales force and no packaging cost. A done deal! The entrepreneur has leapt into the marketplace for rock-bottom dollar, very little risk and tremendous up-side potential.

This book will save individuals and small businesses countless hours in research and trial and error. It unscrambles the new and dynamic telecommunications world, which is so daunting to many people.

The book describes the home shopping system, profiles the channels and lists their "station buyers," those top personnel responsible for procuring product to air. It explains how best to submit a product to station buyers, how to fill out their forms and how to protect a new idea from exploitation. *How To Make Big Money on TV* recommends persistent communication. Once you've cemented a deal with the station, this manual will guide you through manufacturing, assembly, packaging and shipping. As a bonus, it also explains when and how to use infomercials. In addition, Chapter 9, "Creating New Products for TV Using Mind Maps," shows inventors how to hone products that sell.

Home shopping is an extraordinary marketing tool. Last year, in just ten 15-minute shows, I sold more than a half million dollars of product on QVC. Although I have been in sales my whole life, this experience turned my concept of retail delivery upside down. I know home shopping is revolutionizing the marketplace and this book tells how you can take advantage of these new opportunities.

Information Is Power

You've probably heard the old saying, "Information is power." Understanding the information is critical to any endeavor. In an effort to understand high technology, we deal with the triple challenge of complexity, speed and changeability.

The home shopping world is both intricate and hurried; moreover, it is tumultuously evolving by the hour. Without information about it, entrepreneurs will be left in the dust behind a terrific opportunity or bumble through a maze of people and procedures, wasting valuable time and money, while their competition blazes easily to market.

We are in the midst of a dramatic change in the marketplace brought about by home shopping channels and the convergence of sales media brought into our homes by computer. New alliances and deals are being made for now and for the future. Use the tools in this book to make sure you are strategically placed to profit from these changes.

What matters is being among the first to process information. Original information, whether presented on a home shopping channel or on the Internet, usually wins because it's on the cutting edge, and has the first visibility. You can achieve this visibility from your own home. This book will give you the edge to compete and win.

CHAPTER 1

What To Do Before You Approach a Home Shopping Channel

Advantages for Small Businesses Using Home Shopping Channels

Home shopping puts small businesses in the fast lane. No matter where your company is located or your product is produced, you can sell *everywhere*. With the benefit of the mass exposure offered over the airwaves, you have the same advantages as does the CEO of a large company—a direct line to the audience, your consumers. When you or your host are on screen, the size of your company is inconsequential. Your product and the speed with which you can meet customer demand are what count.

As home shopping expands, smaller vendors represented on TV are becoming more numerous and influential. Ironically, while the number of channels is increasing and the stations themselves hold more sway, the physical size of vendors is diminishing. More small and moderate-sized vendors will dominate. Companies with only one product now have the same access to consumers as do those selling thousands of products. The stations work symbiotically with these small vendors to optimize viewer services, with the help of computers. Although those smaller companies may not have individual clout of traditional, blue-chip advertisers, all indications are that their televised advertising will prevail and actually increase in impact.

Testing Your Market with Little Cash

In the past, getting a product on the market was very challenging. Added to the development process were the difficult tasks of packaging, test-marketing, wholesaling the commodity to a retailer and advertising. The cost and hassle of these steps, which were merely tangential to the actual commodity, have kept many wonderful products from the consumer. Home shopping changed all this. Now almost any entrepreneur can get a product to mass market quickly and inexpensively.

First, a product can be marketed by a home shopping channel host on television screens across the country, with the vendor paying little or no advertising investment. Second, home shopping sales require no retail printed packaging. A standard UPS-approved generic box is adequate and saves you thousands of dollars in time, artwork and printing. Finally, home shopping is an ideal means to test-market a new product without forking out thousands of dollars. You can submit a product or prototype to station buyers to gauge the interest. If there is enthusiasm, you then gear up for manufacturing, if you have not already. Since the submission process and approval can take anywhere from several weeks to several months, your production can be in place by the time the product hits the tube.

Before the show airs, the home shopping channel will purchase a certain quantity of product, for which the channel agrees to pay by their purchase order, a legal contract.

Setting Goals and Creating Your Time Line

The "Goal-Setting Worksheet" shown in Figure 1.1 outlines the key steps and common time frames for accomplishing a product placement on a home shopping channel.

Station Buyers Know What Clicks

Station buyers, those station employees in charge of procurement, are central to the success of your endeavor. They decide which products click and which do not, and they make final decisions about which products will go on the air. Station management makes sure that station buyers are highly sensitive to viewer expectations. How does management know if they have hired the right person? If they have not hired the right station buyer, viewers will not see anything worth purchasing and will change channels, that's how. This makes a home shopping channel the ultimate test-marketing device. Even large companies use home shopping channels to test a new product. Or they give an "exclusive" to a station before the product goes retail.

Deciding Which Stations To Target

The paths to getting your product on television are numerous. You will have to weigh the advantages and disadvantages

FIGURE 1.1
Goal-Setting Worksheet

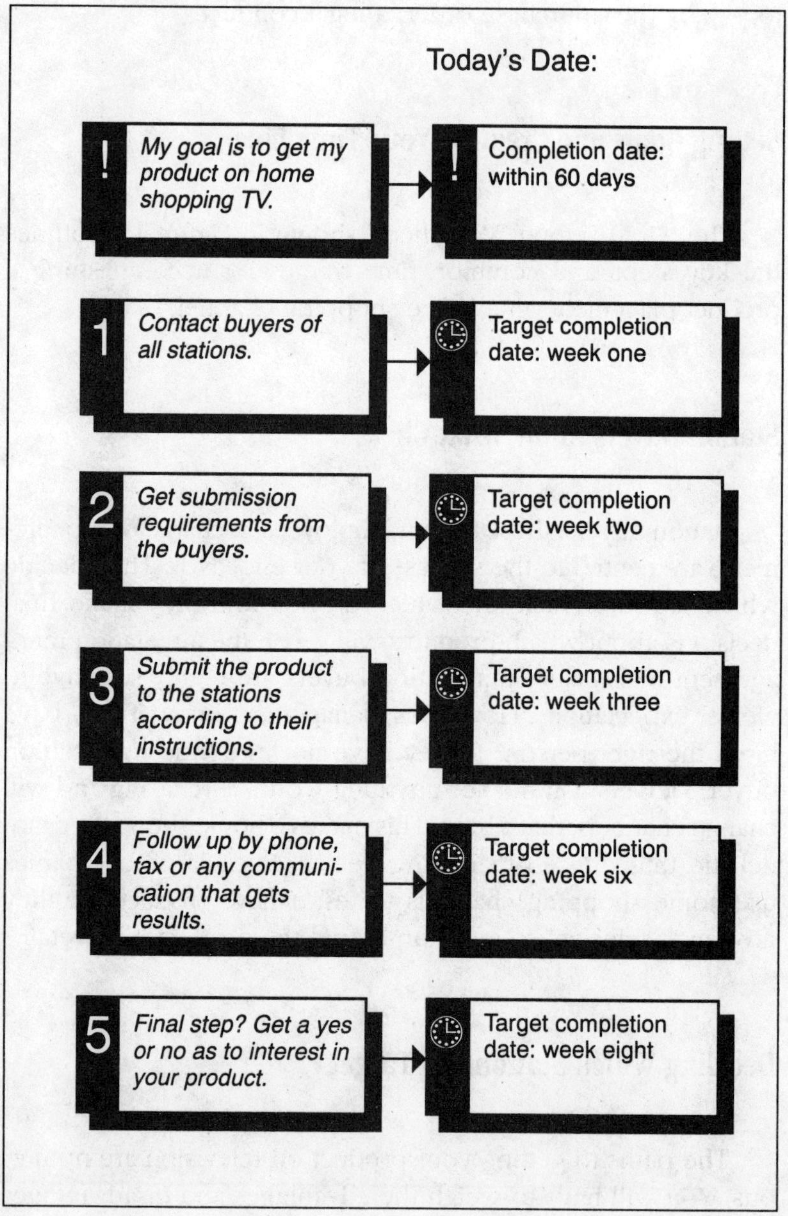
Today's Date:
!
My goal is to get my product on home shopping TV.
!
Completion date: within 60 days
1
Contact buyers of all stations.
Target completion date: week one
2
Get submission requirements from the buyers.
Target completion date: week two
3
Submit the product to the stations according to their instructions.
Target completion date: week three
4
Follow up by phone, fax or any communication that gets results.
Target completion date: week six
5
Final step? Get a yes or no as to interest in your product.
Target completion date: week eight

of large versus small or specialty stations and their buyers against your own manufacturing capability, stock on hand, pricing and so forth. Remember, for every product you have to sell, there are several promising markets.

This book will help you become aware of your options, use the tools you have and narrow those options sensibly. Your goal is to send your product to the particular station and buyer that indicate the most receptivity and enthusiasm.

Often small business people think they should start with the small stations and work their way up. This "stepping-stone approach" is not as sound as it might seem in the home shopping industry. Here's why: Some smaller stations are every bit as particular as large stations about accepting products. Moreover, the marketing of your product has less to do with choosing between large and small stations than with finding those particular stations that most want the product you offer.

Sometimes it will make sense to aim at the larger stations; in other circumstances the smaller or specialty stations will be more appropriate. Which type of station you decide to approach is contingent upon your product, stock on hand, cash flow and manufacturing capabilities. Do not approach large stations unless you can supply the product in a timely fashion!

Identifying Types of Stations

Large Stations

Only two channels reach 40 million viewers each: QVC and HSN (Home Shopping Network). They distinguish themselves not just by virtue of their large viewing audience but also their massive airtime over a large geographic area. Both run 24 hours a day and have a huge following. Working with either QVC or HSN is tantamount to working with ABC, CBS or NBC.

QVC and HSN have a loyal customer base. Viewers are familiar with the programming times, presentation and shopping techniques, and usually know the hosts by name. Obviously, these channels may sell thousands of items per *hour*.

Smaller Stations

As of this writing, no other channels air on as broad a geographical range as QVC and HSN. These smaller stations have fewer than 15 million viewers. Bear in mind though that most can be picked up by satellite dish. The advent of RCA's 18-inch dish, moderately priced at $600, improves the range of the smaller channels. RCA has sold over 1 million of these dishes so far.

Customer loyalty can be just as ardent with small stations as with the large stations. These stations do not necessarily run 24 hours a day, but they may show your product more often than the larger stations, thus selling thousands of items per month.

Specialty Stations

Specialty stations sell high-priced items—often sports-related—or collectibles. The Golf Channel is an example. They may have viewers (potential customers) who are interested in your product because it fits into their category. Specialty stations are becoming more widespread. Their success depends on available airtime, which is limited now but expanding rapidly.

Researching TV Stations

The Appendix will help you get a good start in finding shopping channels. It includes the larger stations such as QVC and HSN as well as top smaller and specialty stations. As we have said, however, the situation is evolving rapidly; sales opportunities are developing daily. *So learn to keep your finger to the pulse of the industry.*

The easiest way to research stations is to watch TV and keep "channel surfing." Keep a running list of infomercial and shopping channel phone numbers.

Call your local stations and ask for their assistance. At times, these stations have direct advertising programs or they may refer you to sources for local programming. In this case, you will contact a company that has bought up large slots of station time that it then sells in increments to people like you.

Several different styles of show format exist. The host format is the most popular. You will also see host plus product creator, host plus demonstration video or host plus product creator plus demonstration video. The best format for you depends a lot on your product.

Keep up with magazine and newspaper articles on the subject. Today, this is easier than ever to do via online companies through Prodigy, America Online or CompuServe. We will talk more about this in Chapter 8, "Selling Online and Other Benefits of the Internet."

The Free Advertising Option

While researching TV stations, you may run into channels who offer *per-inquiry advertising*. Many stations do this now and there will be more in the future. When a station has not sold all of its service, the result is excess airtime. Per-inquiry commercials fill this space. In per-inquiry advertising, a station will run your ad free of charge, then take a percentage of your sales. You do not pay them up front, and they do not pay you. They take a percentage of the gross income. (Let's say you sell your product for $100 and their per-inquiry percentage is 25 percent: They will take $25; you get $75.) By contrast to home shopping channels, the per-inquiry advertising option requires that you provide the commercial.

The typical per-inquiry product sale scenario might run something like this:

Sale price of product	$19.95
Total cost of sale	
Per-inquiry commission (15%)[1]	2.99
Telemarketing (answer call)	1.50
Credit card charges (2.5%)	.50
Product cost	4.00
Total	$ 8.99
Profit (Sale price minus total cost of sale)	$10.96

[1] This varies.

Programming Segments Demystified

During your research, you will find that stations frequently slot programs into specific dates and times, bunching related products into the same time segment. This programming is often listed in TV guides so viewers can plan what they want to watch or tape the show ahead of time.

Segmented programming gives stations with diversified products the same advantages that specialty stations have. More and more stations are moving to segment their programming. Figure 1.2 offers a sample listing of segmented programming.

Determining Product Cycle Time

In sales, there is a sequence that we call the "product cycle." This is a time loop of receiving materials from suppliers, manu-

FIGURE 1.2
Sample Listing of Segmented Programming

Time	Monday	Tuesday	Wednesday
12 A.M.	Gifts	Samples	Presents Practical
1 A.M.	Christmas Shop	Jewelry	Earrings
2 A.M.	Jewelry	Linens	Trends
3 A.M.	Fashions	Rings	Fuzzy Friends
4 A.M.	Diamonds	Executive Gifts	Collectibles
5 A.M.	Gifts for Mom	Jewelry	Presents
6 A.M.	Silver Jewelry	Gifts under $10	Gifts for Dad
7 A.M.	Christmas Special	Gifts for Dad	Western Wear

facturing, packaging, inventory warehousing, shipping and sales that precedes reimbursement. Every product must move through this cycle to achieve profitability. The shorter the cycle time, the more profit to your company. And, of course, the more times you complete the cycle, the more rapidly you perfect it. Figures 1.3 and 1.4 illustrate two different ways of viewing the product cycle time.

In traditional sales, there are many unrelated customers, many transactions. The advent of home shopping bulks all those customers. You target the station buyer, get an order, manufacture your product and deliver it. There is no retail packaging. Shipping is to one, or at most a few, locations. Fewer people are in the loop. It takes much less time to complete a product cycle, because home shopping involves one single process instead of numerous separate ones.

The advantages to the shortened cycle time are obvious. You can use more energy to streamline your manufacturing and

FIGURE 1.3
Product Cycle Time

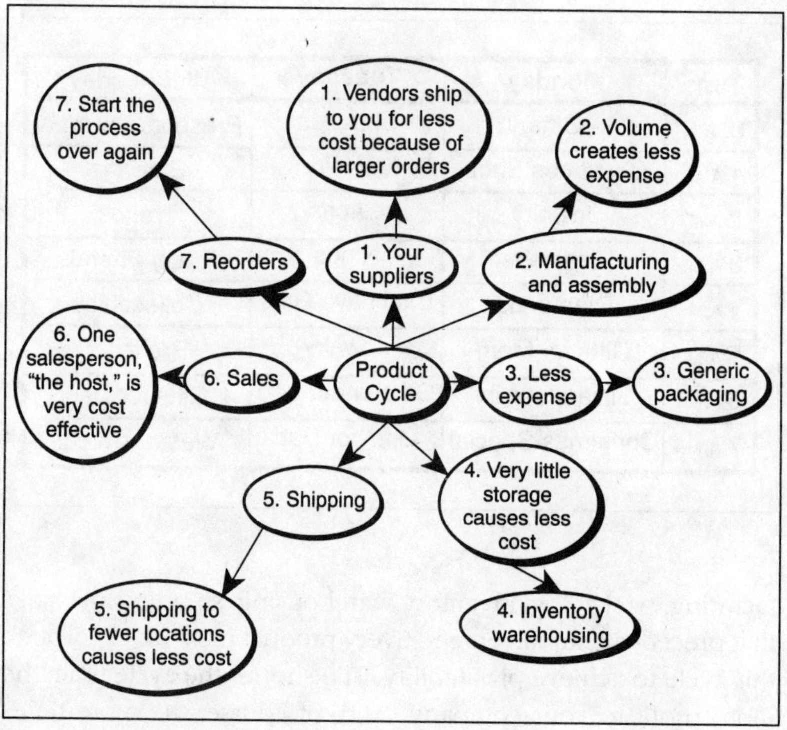

delivery fulfillment process. This will shorten your cycle time even further and make profitability more frequent.

Once you have had sales on a home shopping channel, you will probably want the cycle restructured and streamlined as in "7. Reorders," described in the section that follows. This will also lower costs.

A note of caution: You must always be able to deliver and make sure your suppliers deliver to you! If you lose your sale, you may not get a second chance. Your product development cycles must be completed on time.

FIGURE 1.4
Product Cycle Time

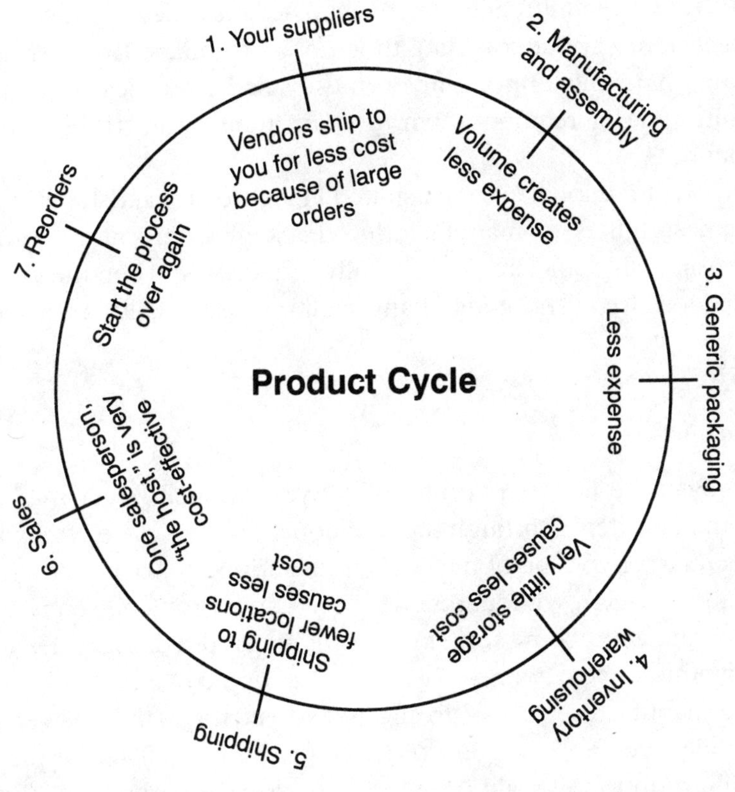

Depending on your manufacturing time, everything could start with the sale! We will need to develop an entirely new set of methods as befits this entirely new set of circumstances. When the cycle isn't moving it ceases to exist as anything but potential, at least until it is allowed to move again!

Honing the Product Cycle for Home Shopping

Prior to home shopping, it was virtually impossible for the individual, entrepreneur or inventor to get a new product on television without spending thousands of dollars. Home shopping opens this opportunity to these smaller businesses; at the same time, it requires them to adapt their cycle to fit a new routine.

The traditional cycle illustrated in Figures 1.3 and 1.4 moves from suppliers to manufacturing, packaging, inventory warehousing, shipping, sales and finally to reorders, when the cycle repeats. Home shopping changes all this, especially in the "reorder" step.

Suppliers

Because home shopping offers you a much larger market than that offered through the traditional product cycle, you will need larger volume of materials from suppliers. To get into this higher echelon without incurring cash flow problems, consider ordering with sliding scale pricing and staggered delivery. Here's how this strategy works: (1) get a price for 5,000 units; (2) ask if the manufacturer can ship the units over time (the answer is usually "yes"); (3) if you do not order the full 5,000, the price will go up to the scale on which you do order, say 2,500 units versus 5,000.

Manufacturing

You have several options from which to choose:

- Do all manufacturing yourself.
- Do part of it, such as assembly or packaging.

- Do none of it and contract a fulfillment house to do all the work and shipping.

Obviously, if you opt to do all the manufacturing, you will make more money and have additional cost for the items you farm out. Most companies, however, get supplies, parts and raw materials from outside suppliers. A fulfillment house will do all of the work for you for a price. This choice is great where pricing is reasonable, especially if you have one product and other full-time obligations

Volume results in less expense. The more frequently a process is done, the faster and easier it becomes. Regardless of how much manufacturing you do, the volume factor will apply.

Packaging

Most home shopping channels require only generic (plain) packaging.

You can forgo all the time and expense of retail packaging development and manufacturing—procedures such as photos, artwork, package design, advertising agencies, packaging and printing.

Make sure that your packaging meets the standards of the United Parcel Service (UPS). If your packaging is not UPS approved, you will have to put your product in a master carton (for each individual unit) to ship UPS.

Inventory Warehousing

Ideally, you are working with on-time delivery—where your products are made after the purchase order is received—so your product should require little inventory or warehousing. When the order is complete, the trucks roll in, and out rolls the product for delivery to the station or the customer, depending on the deal you have structured with the station. This may not be feasible with products that have a larger manufacturing time frame.

Shipping

Since you are shipping volumes of product to one location (or a few), the cost goes down dramatically. There will also be considerable savings in time.

Sales

Hey, one host for one million viewers! With home shopping sales, you have the customer in your pocket. The savings in time and sales costs are gargantuan.

Reorders

The cycle starts all over again.

Have you heard the phrase, "Nothing happens until there is a sale"? With home shopping, this saying has added significance. Suppose your salesperson gives you a reorder for 2,000 units. Now sales becomes number one in your "cycle," suppliers become number two, manufacturing becomes number three, packaging becomes number four, inventory warehousing becomes number five, shipping becomes number six and reorders remain the seventh step.

To reduce negative cash flow, tie your materials suppliers to the purchase order: They get paid when you do. Suppliers with whom you have done business should be particularly open to this kind of structure. Incorporate a clause into contracts that basically tells materials suppliers to "deliver on time or else." You have to *demand* this.

Instead of trying to fit the new delivery system into an existing organizational structure, restructure your company so that you can introduce new products with lightning speed. This usually translates into less middle management, fewer marketing expenditures and reduced costs.

When the product cycle starts with the sale, home shopping saves everyone money—viewers, vendors, stations and you!

Overcoming Some Common Misconceptions about Getting into the Home Shopping Market

People who are new to sales or even just new to home shopping (and that includes just about everyone) can be easily discouraged by any one of many erroneous blanket statements. Even if your product is already in the marketplace, sales can slow down or otherwise be undermined by misconceptions.

You may be told any one of the following:

1. Your category of product is not selling well right now.
2. You have no previous sales history.
3. If it is in discount stores, we do not want it.
4. We want an exclusive! That is the deal.
5. You cannot get the product sold yourself. You need us.
6. It is difficult to get on TV.

There may be some truth to these statements, truth kept alive by the people who repeat or hear them frequently. Nonetheless, I encourage you to disregard these half-truths. As many, many salespeople know, we all have the power to change or circumvent policies and practices that threaten to impede us. Exceptions are the rule. When people who believe in their product proceed in a business-like manner, everybody benefits—stations, viewers and you, the vendor, alike.

Consider the converse of those statements above:

1. Your category of product may not be selling well right now, because *your* particular product is not part of the spectrum.
2. Each of us has been "in sales" our whole lives. Anyone who has communicated anything has the ability to present a convincing appeal.
3. Your product's presence in discount stores will only augment interest in buying it over television at a reduced price or at more convenience.
4. Same as answer 3.
5. There are always alternatives.
6. It may be difficult to get on TV, but it is not impossible. Many people do it, and more and more will in the future.

Armed with these responses, and with the help of this book and the strength of your own convictions, you will get that product on home shopping channels. Once you hear testimonials from viewers about the worthiness of your product, you will know that it was worth challenging the status quo.

I would be remiss here if I did not mention the possibility of returns. Most channels give shoppers an unconditional 30-day money-back guarantee. The station charges these returns back to you.

There is no shipping charge for returns. In most cases, the items are in a condition to resell. At our company, the return rate averages less than 1 percent. However, this varies from product to product. On the up-side, the station is responsible for all bad debt.

The Importance of Tracking the Trends: Recent News

Home shopping is in constant flux. I cannot emphasize enough the importance of staying informed. Newspaper and magazine articles are your greatest resource; you can access these most easily through the Internet, which will be discussed further in Chapter 8.

As you can see from the following examples, new developments will help you shape your product and direct it more effectively to the broadest audience base.

Mediamaxx, Inc. This company announces that "Bookview," a television show that highlights new books, Bibles, videos and software, will premiere on cable, local broadcast and network affiliate stations during February 1996. The show aims to broaden the exposure of Christian products beyond the current radio and print media. Executive producers Dale Hanson Bourke and Bruce R. Barbour see the show as an opportunity to reach out to people who are interested in Christian bookstores. At the same time, they will raise the visibility of products to the broader Christian market.

The show itself demonstrates products, shows clips from videos and provides an opportunity for the authors or hosts to discuss the books and other materials. During commercial breaks, they provide product ordering information.

Discovery Communications. This company reports that the Discovery Channel Latin America, launched on February 7, 1994, is available with a choice of three audio feeds—English, Spanish or Portuguese. The Discovery Channel launched throughout Asia on January 17, 1994. Airing 24 hours per day in English, the show will soon include Mandarin and Bahasa-Indonesian subtitles. The network will add other languages as the need arises.

Home Shopping Network. This company announced that it plans to introduce a new national electronic retailing network, TSM (Television Shopping Mall), designed to position traditional retailers, catalogers and consumer product manufacturers on the electronic "information superhighway."

TSM can accommodate 35 participants for 70 two-hour shows per week. Remaining hours will be devoted to "Home Shopping Spree," Home Shopping Network's overnight service. They anticipate initial distribution to be three million cable households within five years. The show will be live, taped or both. Contracts with TSM programmers will be for one year initially, with options to renew for longer periods.

TSM will have its own look, personality and identity, separate and distinct from Home Shopping Network's "Home Shopping Club." Merchandisers will create their own TSM "stores," each achieving desired individual looks and sensibilities.

MTV channel announced the inclusion of a Music Shopping Network targeted at MTV fans and selling music-related paraphernalia such as recorded music, concert tickets and souvenirs. It will air on MTV and VH-1, as well as Nickelodeon's "Nick at Nite." These shows will have a look and feel all their own. They have already developed environments that are uniquely conducive to marketing music. Part of the impetus for launching the new service is an increase in catalog sales of musical merchandise. If all goes well, MTV may launch a whole separate music shopping network.

Taking Advantage of TV for Market Research

One of your greatest information resources is television itself. Unfortunately, few people know how to take full advantage of the TV treasure trove. Have you ever said, "If only I had known that show was on TV"? Have you ever wished you could locate specific television programs by subject? Have you ever just wanted to know what was airing without having to sift through all the listings? Then check out TVNow, a new personal television guide from the Software-of-the-Month Club.

Club members can use their computers for research and sourcing. TVNow has comprehensive listings of movies, series, musicals, sports, specials and shows for more than 70 national cable channels, covering all time zones in the United States. Its powerful search features let you search your subject by actor name, program types, team name, program ratings, title and many other criteria which could bear on your research.

Here's an opportunity for designing a guide that corresponds to whatever field you want. You can actually program the guide to scan only those stations you receive in your time zone, as well as any other stations of interest. Use your VCR to tape the shows if you plan to be out.

As a member of the Software-of-the-Month Club, you will receive the latest schedule monthly on a 3.5-inch high-density disk. The first month's disk includes the TVNow software. It's easy to install and easy to use.

To contact the Software-of-the-Month Club, call 619-930-7301 or fax them at 619-930-7383.

CHAPTER
2

Preparing Your Product To Submit

Does Your Product Click?

A few years ago, early home shopping channels discovered the profitability of offering items with broad appeal that could be ordered conveniently from viewers' homes. They started with simple selling techniques offering jewelry, housewares, and health and beauty products. Today, everything from dolls to sophisticated electronics is being sold over the airwaves. Large Fortune 500 companies regularly sell back-to-back with individual inventors such as myself.

The key here is the product. Great products do not require a snow job to sell. Many products can and will sell very well on home shopping channels, as you have probably already heard about or seen. Is your product conducive to selling over television? Anyone, no matter how small, may submit their product to stations for consideration. Even if you are only a one-person company, if you have a good product, have at it!

Timing Your Seasonal Products

From the station buyer's viewpoint in particular, some products are seasonal. What clicks for winter may not click in the summer months. For example, snow removal equipment, back-to-school items and swim gear are going to be hotter properties during certain times of year. It takes anywhere from two to three months to get your product approved, shipped and on the air. (A simple product may take less time than a more complicated one.) You have to gauge your product's seasonability, create a schedule and get it to the station buyer at the appropriate time.

This can be tricky. For instance, a baseball bat is a spring item, but it may start selling in the Sunbelt in January. Do not assume that the station buyer knows this. You may wish to point out in your submission that "There is more baseball equipment sold in January than in any other month. September is number two."

While we are on the subject of seasonal products, let me throw you a curve. One large shopping channel had "Christmas in July," a show for early-bird buyers. Do not presume too much about seasonal products; yours could fit a special niche. Ask.

Asking the Crucial Three Questions

If you can answer the following three questions with a positive response, your product is headed in the right direction for home shopping appeal.

1. *Is your product unique?* A unique product narrows the competition, and keeps the interest of the viewer. Buyers like this trait.
2. *Does your product have mass appeal?* Mass appeal virtually ensures acceptance of a product. This is why products used often in the house or yard and on your car are so much easier to get on the air. For example, the Flowbee, which cuts your hair and eliminates the mess, has mass appeal. A family of four uses Flowbee an average of 48 times per year, saving countless dollars for the customer. That's "mass appeal" and value.
3. *Does your product have quality and value?* Stations monitor quality very closely. If there is no quality, *forget it.*

Use the 12-item rating guide in Figure 2.1 to determine the likelihood of your product succeeding on TV.

Creating a Persuasive Product Description

In order to make a clear presentation to station buyers, you need to create an easy-to-understand and persuasive description of your product. Although this sounds easy to do, it's not. It is usually the result of hard work and concrete thinking, combined with a lot of input from others. Make sure the written or audiovisual material you submit makes sense and entices first the buyer, then the public, to experience the product first hand. Quality photographs are a must. Before sending anything off, get feedback from people who do not know the product.

For a product description example, see Figure 2.2, a detailed description of one of my current products, "Virtual Baseball." This sample illustrates the enormous amount of planning that goes into a product presentation. You will see the many product benefits I conceived to help build a vision I could promote.

FIGURE 2.1
Rating Your Product

GUIDE ONLY
Can Your Product Succeed on TV?

ITEM	Strong (10 pts.)	Good (7 pts.)	Weak (4 pts.)	Rating
1	Markup is 5 to 1 or better.	Markup is less than 5 to 1 but more than 3 to 1.	Less than 3 to 1 markup.	
2	Demonstrated mass-market appeal.	Has solid sales research.	Has very little research.	
3	Blue-collar appeal.	Appeals to educated customer.	Has very narrow appeal.	
4	Easily demonstrable (e.g., kitchen gadget).	Can't be fully demonstrated (e.g., success item, audiotape).	Difficult to demonstrate.	
5	Proven retail or direct sales.	Similar to a successful product.	Is untested.	
6	Existing testimonials.	Testimonials can be gathered quickly.	Testimonials may be difficult.	
7	Ratio of value to price is very attractive.	Value is good but price is relatively high.	Price is high, value low.	
8	Strong focus group response.	Has moderate focus group response.	Has weak focus group response.	
9	Price is $19.95 or less/or lead generator.	Price is $49.95 or less.	Price is over $49.95.	
10	Fulfills dream, makes life better.	Has solid perceived value.	Has little perceived value.	
11	Good upsell or backend potential.	Has limited upsell or backend potential.	Has little or no upsell or backend potential.	
12	Makes excellent 30- or 60-second commercial.	Best in 1- to 2-minute commercial.	Best in print media only.	
			Total Rating Points	

Strong = 94–120 pts.; Good = 70–94 pts.; Weak = 69 or below

Hiring a Professional Broker

You can hire a professional broker to submit new products to stations. Find brokers through the stations or infomercial companies.

If you are considering doing business through a broker, you can use the following pros and cons to help you weigh the worth of this type of agenting for your particular situation. Remember, the situation is the boss. I suggest you interview several brokers, and check references, before you make a decision.

Pros

- A broker knows the system.
- A broker knows the buyers.
- Usually, the broker lives close to the station.
- A broker knows how to negotiate a good price.
- A broker saves you time.

Cons

- A broker usually charges 5 percent commission.
- A broker represents more than one product—yours may not be in the forefront.
- You will not be personally in touch with the station—losing a valuable learning experience.
- You may do a better job than a broker.

Pricing Your Product

Pricing is key for products presented on home shopping channels. Typically, buyers strive to get the product for less

FIGURE 2.2
Product Description: "Virtual Baseball"

C 3 D
Sports

2423 Camino Del Rio So. #210
San Diego, CA 92108
619/294-4070

One constant throughout the years has been baseball.

Enclosed please find information on our newly developed product, VIRTUAL BASEBALL. I believe VIRTUAL BASEBALL will be a big hit for the following reasons:

1. It's the first baseball/softball product where interactive play can be done indoors or out. This eliminates the seasonal aspect.

2. It's the first real virtual reality product for baseball/softball.

3. Computerized electronic products are *hot*. VIRTUAL BASEBALL combines training with a computerized electronic game. Physical activity and computer games combine in one great activity. It will succeed for the same reason that fax is more widely used than E-mail—*touch!* Playing with VIRTUAL BASEBALL is the hitter's way of making another hit. Repeat a hit every few seconds and get instant feedback—all by using information formulated in the computerized technology of "Power Hit."

4. It is not available at this time for purchase anywhere else. This is an exclusive.

5. Customers can use their own bat. This eliminates matching bat size to the customer. Any size bat works.

6. The demographics of this product are far reaching. There are 30 million baseball players (3.5 million new players per year), 60 million softball players and potential interest for nonbaseball or softball players because of the game aspect.

7. VIRTUAL BASEBALL can be used by anyone from age 3 to a pro. Why? Because players can use their own bats, and because the computerized electronic "Power Hit" can be regulated so that anyone can hit a home run. All you need to do is set the controls.

FIGURE 2.2, *continued*
Product Description: "Virtual Baseball"

8. This "Power Hit" regulating device means that mom, dad, brother, sister and grandparent can play baseball on equal terms. As each comes up to bat, "Power Hit" can be set—low power for the child, higher power for the adult. *Equivalence* makes this an especially appealing family game.

Please call me at your earliest convenience, since we would like to make you the first to show this product. Time is of the essence. Hot potential products usually do not stay secret, but we'd like VIRTUAL BASEBALL to remain so long enough to advance your interests and ours.

Sincerely,

Craig Daugard
President

Enclosures:

<u>Product Contents:</u>

1. 35' steel plastic-covered cable
2. Pitch stick
3. 1 plastic baseball, 1 plastic softball
4. 1 bolt & nut
5. Computerized electronic "Power Hit"
6. Handle
7. 3 lock loops
8. Full instructions and hitting tips

("Power Hit" works on 4 rechargeable batteries (not included) UL-approved.)

FIGURE 2.2, *continued*
Product Description: "Virtual Baseball"

VIRTUAL BASEBALL . . . Just Like Reality

VIRTUAL BASEBALL is more than a game. It is a training device. And while players learn about hitting a baseball, they will also gain confidence and perspective on the nature of competence.

Consisting of a cable line, pitch stick, balls (baseball and softball) and a revolutionary electronic pitching device, "Power Hit," VIRTUAL BASEBALL requires no playing field and no teammates. Whether the player is 3 years old or a professional athlete, he or she can play VIRTUAL BASEBALL anywhere, with the player's own bat.

What a training device! Using far less space and time than conventional methods, VIRTUAL BASEBALL combines computerization with electronics to match the skills of individual players.

We have divided the game into two parts—offensive and defensive. While the nature of the game has not changed, the player's perception will. The defense of traditional baseball is condensed in time and space with the cable line and "Power Hit" pitching device. The cable line limits the action to where it counts. "Power Hit" puts the game or training into sync with the player's offensive ability. This is what makes VIRTUAL BASEBALL so effective and fun. The player's expanded consciousness leads to better training.

Sometimes the real story is not about the new product; it is about the effect on the millions of people who use it. Athletes are an elite species. In grade school, we all get to play. In high school or organized team sports, 8-10 percent get to compete. In college, less than 1 percent play. What has happened? Those who lack offensive ability have been severed from the action. Inexpensive products such as this that help develop offensive skills (the fun part of sports) help everyone get their fair shot at being among the elite.

Those who make a practice of remembering successes and minimizing their failures will begin to experience more success than they thought possible. But the situation is somewhat different in physical learning. In a typical baseball-playing learning scenario, a player will at first miss the ball many more times than he will hit it. With practice, his misses will

FIGURE 2.2, *continued*
Product Description: "Virtual Baseball"

gradually diminish; the hits will come more frequently. If mere repititions were the key to improving skill, his practice should make him more expert at missing the ball than hitting it. However, even though the misses outnumber the hits, the player hits the ball more successfully because the mind and body remember, reinforce and concentrate on the successful attempts rather than the misses, reinforced by calls of "foul ball," "1st," "2nd," "3rd" and "home run."

Because it can be gauged to a player's level of competence, VIRTUAL BASEBALL provides many more successful attempts in a shorter period of time. It builds confidence the same way, through mental and physical imagery.

The benefit to kids is evident. But what about adults? Adults are all too given to relying exclusively on their minds. They have already been separated from athletic endeavor at an early age. Now the only training taking place is in their racing minds. But grownup toys can awaken an element of play in all of us. Correctly harnessed, VIRTUAL BASEBALL can transcend its game status and actually build confidence as it amplifies athletic ability.

Virtual extensions of our human abilities promote nonlinear perceptual exploration and subverbal inquiry by facilitating high levels of intuitive interaction and higher degrees of sensorial involvement. The use of nonorthodox equipment often yields surprising insight.

Competition is a very powerful tool. Desire for results fosters motivation. Motivation, in turn, hones attentiveness. When a player is attentive, he or she will make all the right moves. The state of mind that anticipates a correct swing is trained attentiveness.

The rapid succession of pitches—one every six seconds—helps the player learn through experience and immediate feedback from computerized electronics. The learning time will be shortened dramatically. The practice will help the player in actual game situations.

Along these lines, training situations with VIRTUAL BASEBALL optimize our brain's tendency to fill in missing experience. Therefore, when a player hits a home run, he or she will acquire the confidence to visualize being at the playing field hitting a home run.

FIGURE 2.2, *continued*
Product Description: "Virtual Baseball"

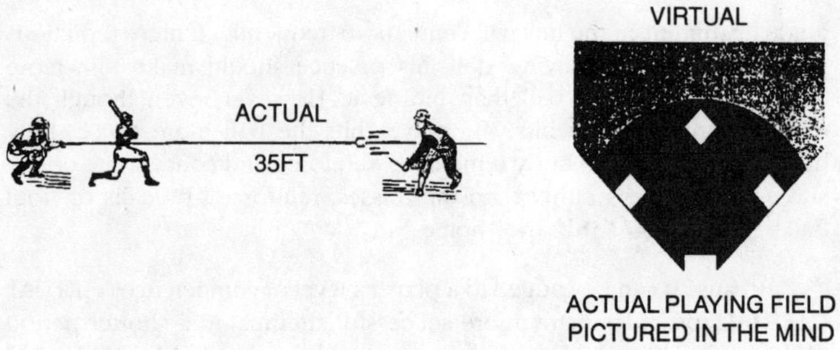

Depicted above, the offense's objective is to hit the ball. It is the pitch that controls the interactivity between the batter and the ball. The batter hits the ball with the bat reacting to the pitch every six seconds. The space is shortened by 30' to 1' with a batter's box. The swing, which is guided by eye-to-hand coordination (mental-physical combination) creates the hit. All this takes place in space and time, both abbreviated, but both "actually" experienced through mental imagery.

Key points of VIRTUAL BASEBALL

1. Self-supervised learning is possible.
2. Repetition over time builds muscle memory.
3. "Power Hit," the computerized electronics in the game, is programmed with the ability to respond to the power in the hit, ranging from foul ball to home run. And it is adjustable to age and ability.
4. VIRTUAL BASEBALL makes training in the framework of a game more engaging than the real world.
5. VIRTUAL BASEBALL can be more intriguing than actual baseball or softball because it brings equivalence to the game. Power adjustments may be made to compensate for age and aptitudes so that players can play together on equal terms.
6. It is quick and easy to set up, even for one person.
7. If the cable is set up between two poles, a person can play solo.
8. By adding simple programs and simple parts, the player may play a more challenging game.
9. Improvements made in batting skills may translate into better performance and raised consciousness in other parts of the player's life.
10. VIRTUAL BASEBALL takes a routine and repetitive task—practice—and makes it interesting. This is crucial to keeping the player training on his or her own. Fun is key.

than wholesale so they can price it to sell for less than the standard recommended retail price.

When you factor in the savings of sales made on television over standard sales, it justifies the lower pricing. Remember, you benefit from the following:

1. Generic packaging, which costs less than typical retail packaging
2. Shipping a large volume of product to just one location, which lowers your cost
3. Mass exposure and free advertising
4. Accessory sales in parts or replacements that will help generate more profits
5. The boost into the retail market, without advertising and other marketing expenses, that television sales give you
6. Referral sales generated from people who buy the product from a home shopping channel

Both you the vendor and the station make a profit.

There is a downside to pricing your product lower for screen sales. Unfortunately, the consumer will perceive that as its retail price. If it is too low, it could cause problems when you begin presenting your product to retail stores. On the other hand, if it is too high, you may never get on television at all. Pricing your product for television can be a harrowing tightrope walk of a decision. Weigh all aspects and hire outside consultants or a broker if you think you need them.

Selling Your Product Along with a Video Demo

Many products can be enhanced and perceived value increased by selling the product with accompanying demonstration videotape. You may have the type of product that will cause more of a stir with videotaped instructions showing various ways to use it. I have seen videos in everything from spaghetti makers to health training devices. When appropriate, video training or instructions can help raise the perceived value of the product. The video itself fits the electronics trend. It also helps sell the product on TV, since the station will probably use excerpts from it to aid the program host in selling the product.

This will inflate the value of your product without costing all that much more. Video duplication costs are inexpensive, if your orders are large. I duplicated 3,000 videos for a cost of 87 cents each.

Protecting Your New Product

Patents

If I came up with a great idea and knew that I could produce several thousand of them easily and quickly, I would not hesitate. I would start the submission process to home shopping channels right away. However, I highly recommend that any product be as fully protected as possible. I would make sure I had as many photos and diagrams and as much documentation as necessary. Then I would apply for a patent.

In Figure 2.3, you'll see a sample patent goals checklist and time line. A blank patent goals checklist is in Appendix 2 for your use. You should initiate the patent process as soon as possible, since the product should not be described in a public publication, publicly used, sold or even offered for sale before the application. The patent process usually takes 18 months. To initiate the protection process, submit a disclosure statement that is available from the federal government (see Figure 2.4) with a $10 fee to the U.S. Patent Office. This document is dated, time-stamped and kept on file for two years. *Warning*: This is not patent coverage. It only shows when the idea began. This information may be used later when the patent is filed.

The Patent and Trademark Office maintains a phone line designated for general assistance on patent protection. Use it:

Commissioner of Patents and Trademarks
U.S. Department of Commerce
Patent and Trademark Office
Washington, DC 20231
703-308-HELP

Unless inventors are familiar with patent law and Patent and Trademark Office practice, they can get into considerable difficulties. I *highly* recommend consulting a patent attorney. A regular communication channel to a good patent attorney or technology agent is a resource that every product developer will use over and again.

Access to good advice is essential for protecting your product; this is especially true when you face that initial need for a patent, design protection or trademark. Background searches in patent and trademark fields are crucial to the product development process, and applications for registration need to be done as promptly and economically as possible.

Fortunately, the same communications revolution that the Internet represents also provides the resources for you to form that professional relationship. One plugged-in resource that we have learned about is the Intellectual Property Institute and its national network of patent professionals—IPINet—linked in cyberspace with each other and their clients.

Conceived as a virtual corporation for legal and product development service, IPI is committed to using modern communications technology to serve inventors and product managers faster and more effectively. A variety of information resources are available from IPI at no charge, including patent specification worksheets and advice on creating a strong trademark.

FIGURE 2.3
Patent Goals Checklist

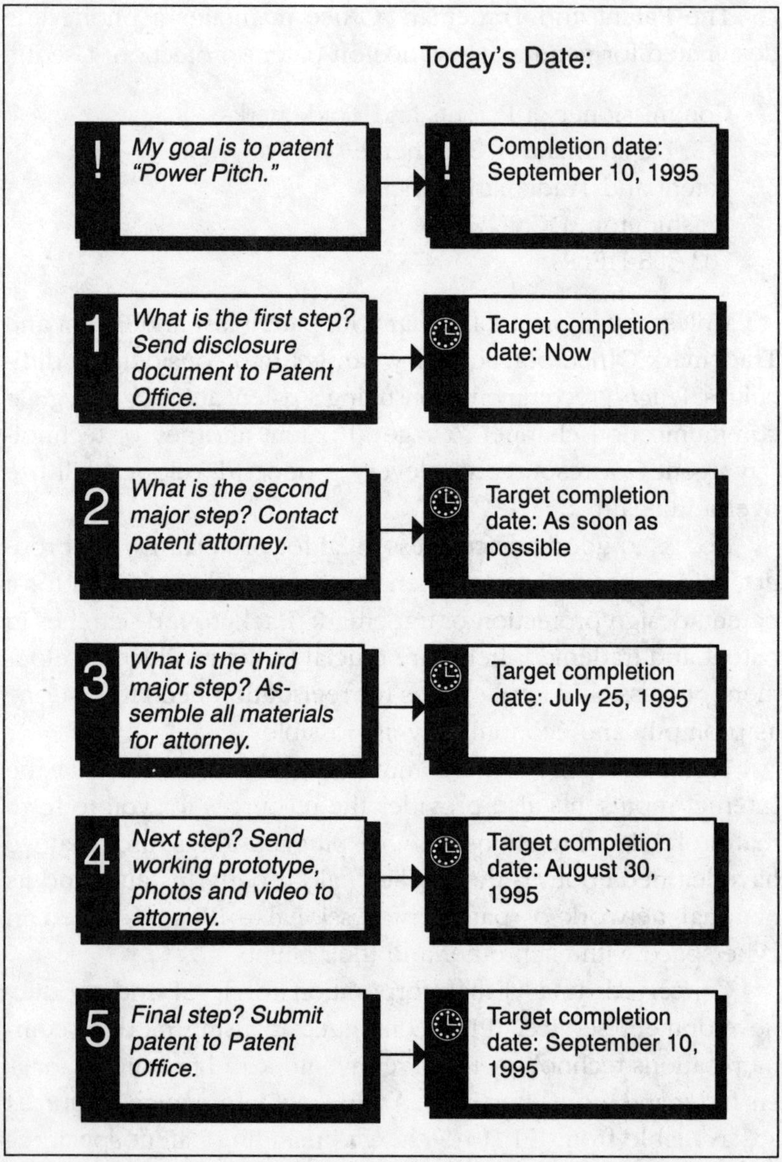

FIGURE 2.4
Sample Disclosure Document

Box DD
Commissioner of Patents and Trademarks
Washington, District of Columbia 20231

Request for Participation in Disclosure Document Program

Disclosure of Your Name(s) *Craig Daugard*

Entitled: Title of Disclosure *Power Pitch*

Sir:

Attached are two copies of a disclosure of my above-entitled invention (consisting of *2* sheets of written description and separate drawings or photos), a $*10* check, a stamped, addressed return envelope, and duplicates.

The undersigned respectfully requests that this disclosure be accepted and retained for two years (or longer if it is later referred to in a paper filed in a patent application) under the Disclosure Document Program and that the enclosed duplicate of this letter be date stamped, numbered and returned in the envelope also enclosed.

The undersigned understands that (1) this disclosure document is neither a patent application nor a substitute for one, (2) its receipt date will not become the effective filing date of a later-filed patent application, (3) it will be retained for two years and then destroyed unless it is referred to in a patent application, (4) this two-year retention period is not a "grace period" during which a patent application can be filed without loss of benefits. (5) In addition to this document, proof of diligence in building and testing the invention, and/or filing a patent application on the invention, may be vital in the case of an interference, and in other situations, (6) if such building and testing is done, signed, and dated, records of such should additionally be made and these should be witnessed and dated by disinterested individuals (not the PTO), and (7) if any public use or sale of the invention is made in the U.S., or any publication is made

FIGURE 2.4, *continued*
Sample Disclosure Document

anywhere, no valid patent can be granted on the invention unless a patent application is filed on it within one year of any such public use, sale or publication, regardless of the filing date of this Disclosure Document.

Very respectfully,

Craig Daugard	
Signature of Inventor	Signature of Joint Inventor
Craig Daugard	
c/o (Print Name)	Print Name
2423 Camino Del Rio So. #210	
Address	Address
San Diego, CA 92108	

Note: Be sure you follow the first paragraph to perfection.

Have you ever had the experience of telephone tag with a lawyer when you need information right away? Who hasn't? You will appreciate the ability to send a query to your IPI patent attorney by E-mail 24 hours a day and receive a reply by the next morning. Moreover, direct file transfers to your computer make the uncertainty of sending legal drafts by the U.S. Postal Service a thing of the past.

IPI's team network handles most transactions, including patent searches and patent applications. The agents themselves have offices throughout the U.S. and are available in many areas for on-site consultation when necessary.

For information on the Intellectual Property Institute and IPINet services, contact:

Intellectual Property Institute
3639 Midway Drive, Suite 142
San Diego, CA 92110
Phone/fax 619-222-1387
E-mail: ipi@aol.com

Online computer services that will save you money and time are as follows:

- CLAIMS (Class Assignee Index Method Search)
  IFTI/Plenum Dirata Corp.
  910-291-0068
  CLAIMS includes three separate databases that list more than 2.3 million U.S. patents issued by the U.S. Patent and Trademark Office.
- LEXPAT
  LEXIS-NEXIS
  800-227-4908
  LEXPAT features full text coverage of all utility patents issued by the U.S. Patent and Trademark Office since 1975, and all plant and design patents issued since December 1976.
- Patent Status File
  Rapid Patent Service
  This service lists a score of post-issue actions that affect U.S. patents dating back to 1973.
- Trademarkscan-U.S.
  Thomson & Thomson
  617-479-1600
  Trademarkscan-U.S. lists all trademarks and service marks issued by or applied for at the U.S. Patent and Trademark Office.
- U.S. Copyrights
  U.S. Copyright Office
  202-707-3000

This database contains details on all active copyright and mask-work registrations filed at the U.S. Copyright Office.

- U.S. Patent Fulltext
  U.S. Patent and Trademark Office
  703-557-4636
  This service features full-text coverage of U.S. patents issued by the U.S. Patent and Trademark Office.
- U.S. Patents
  Derwent, Inc.
  703-790-0400
  This service includes extensive patent data, with complete front-page information and claims on all U.S. patents issued from 1971 to the present.

If you put a new product up for sale without filing for a patent, you have one year from the date of the first sale or public showing to file.

If a product is sold without a patent, you may not be able to get foreign patent protection at all. If you do plan to sell a product overseas and to get a patent for another country, you should contact a patent attorney prior to the first public showing or sale. You should also copyright all written and audiovisual materials about the product. This is done through the

Register of Copyrights
Library of Congress
Washington, DC 20559
General copyright information: 202-707-3000
Form hotline: 202-707-9100

Insurance

Stations ask for a $1 million product liability policy, which covers the product if, due to faulty manufacturing or poor design, it causes injury or harm. Any insurance source can supply this policy.

In addition, if your product does well on television, you are going to need protection from piracy. Two agencies help minimize the cost of litigation. The Intellectual Product Insurance Services works just like an insurance agency. You pay premiums annually and they pay for litigation up to the policy limits.

By contrast, the Patent Protection Institute works like a bank. They finance patent enforcement litigation in exchange for a percentage of recovery or a percentage of your patent. What this means is that they own a percentage of the patent and therefore receive a percentage of the proceeds after product sales.

- Intellectual Property Insurance Services Corp.
  10503 Timberwood Circle
  Louisville, KY 40223
  800-537-7863
- Patent Protection Institute
  P. O. Box 1334
  Ross, CA 94957
  415-499-5700

Inventors' Organizations

In addition, inventor's clubs, associations and innovation centers can be valuable resources. For their locations, contact the following organizations:

- Inventors Submission Corp.
  8898 Clairemont Mesa Blvd., Suite C
  San Diego, CA 92123
  619-278-9925
- Inventors Workshop International
  7332 Mason Avenue
  Canoga Park, CA 91306-2822
  818-340-4268

- Minnesota Inventors Congress
  P.O. Box 71
  Redwood Falls, MN 56283-0071
  507-637-2344
- National Congress of Inventor Organizations (NCIO)
  727 North 600 West
  Logan, UT 84321
  801-753-0888
- United Inventors Association of the United States of America (UIA-USA)
  P.O. Box 50305
  St. Louis, MO 63105 (stamped, self-addressed envelope required)

Books on Protecting Your Invention

- Debelak, Don. *How To Bring a Product to Market for Less Than $5,000*, New York: John Wiley & Sons.
- Foster, Frank H., and Robert L. Shook. *Patents, Copyrights and Trademarks*. New York: John Wiley & Sons.
- Lynn, Gary S. *From Concept to Market*. New York: John Wiley & Sons.
- Mosley, Thomas E. Jr. *Marketing Your Invention*. Chicago: Upstart Publishing, Inc.

Determining Your Product's Classification

Start by determining if your product falls into any standard category. Figure 2.5 features a classification of products stations are seeking. If your product is not listed, don't worry! Call the station to see if there is an interest. Product selection changes every day.

FIGURE 2.5
Product Classification Chart

Jewelry Products
precious metal with gemstones
cubic zirconia jewelry
special accents
neckchains/bracelets
Black Hills gold/silver
costume jewelry
celebrity jewelry
14-karat jewelry
rings
como diamonte
watches

Soft Goods
missy sweaters
coordinates
separates
blazers
shoes
dresses
scarves, belts, accessories
loungewear/lingerie
sport sets
evening wear
suits
men's clothing
outerwear
children's clothing
handbags
full figure
jumpsuits
petites

Hard Goods
video recorders/equipment
answering machines
crafts/hobbies
computers: software/games
audio equipment
memorabilia
cameras/clocks
celebrity audio/video
appliances
musical instruments
fitness equipment
capodiamonte
table top/crystal
kitchen accessories
cookware
domestic/optics
makeup/cosmetics/lifeway
silver plate
diets/over-the-counter medicine
dolls: collectible/toys
Christmas
doll accessories
household/floor care
personal care
miscellaneous electronics
electronic: home/office
telephones
radar detectors/lighting/furniture
fitness/entertainment apparel
televisions
sporting goods
prerecorded audio/video
toys/games
ceramic giftware
luggage/totes/attaché cases
dinner flatware
floor coverings
health care/vitamins
perfume
air/water treatment
hardware/yard/auto/misc.
food products
collectibles/art/seasonal/
stationery/books

Product Information Sheets

When you submit a product to a station, you will be required to fill out a form similar to the samples shown in Figures 2.6–2.8. (These forms are shown strictly as samples. The stations may send or fax you their own form.) Working with this form will help you pull together information and formulate a thorough and enticing description of your product.

FIGURE 2.6
Product Presentation Sheet—Soft Goods Only

Any pictures, catalog or advertisements will be helpful in the decision-making process concerning this offer.

Company Name:	
Company Address:	
Contact:	
Fax #:	Phone #:
Signature:	
Style #:	Size Range:
Color:	Qty:
Description:	
Regular Wholesale:	Retail Value Range:
Cost to Station:	Fiber Content:
Is This a Closeout?	Date Available To Ship:

FIGURE 2.7
Company Information

Your Name:	Title:
Company Name:	
Address:	
Phone #:	Fax #:
Manufacturer of Product:	
Model #:	Style #:
Suggested List Price:	Cost:
Terms of Payment:	
Freight:	
Description of Product (Including Measurements—Height, Weight, Length, Width, Color, etc.):	
Is Product Shippable UPS?	
Warranty (If Any):	
Best Price with Maximum Order:	
Number of Units Available Monthly?	
Quantity on Hand?	
Has Your Product Been on TV Before?	
If Yes, What TV Stations?	
If Items Are Being Sold Retail, Where and For What?	
What Is Return Procedure?	
Do You Have Liability Insurance and How Much?	

FIGURE 2.8
Product Presentation—Hard Goods and Jewelry

Attach picture, catalog, price list, advertisements, retail verification (preferably something with the full suggested list). Include any paperwork available. A copy of instructions and warranty must accompany this presentation.

Full Suggested Retail:	
Regular Wholesale:	
Highest Retail Price:	Where:
Price List Attached:	
Avg. Retail Range:	Is This a Closeout?
Quantity Available:	Lead Time To Ship:
Item:	
Description & Features:	
Model #:	Manufacturer:
End User to Mfg. Return Policy:	
Is There a Rebate with This Item?	
Mfg. Address (For Customer Inquiry):	
Rebate Amount:	
Mfg. Customer Service Phone #:	
Warranty Length:	
Warranty Address:	

FIGURE 2.8, *continued*
Product Presentation—Hard Goods and Jewelry

Where Is Warranty Card Located?		
Are Instructions Enclosed with Each Piece?		
Is There Anything Else Enclosed with This Item?		
Color:		
Vendor's Name:		
Vendor's Address:		
Contact:	Fax #:	Phone #:
Weight Each:		
How Is Each One Packaged?		
Case Pack:	Case Weight:	Case Color:
Terms of Payment:		
UL Listed:		
Shipping Point:	Prepaid Freight:	
FOB:	Duty Rate (Where Applicable):	
Quantity on 48' Trailer:	Quantity on 40' Container:	
Amount of Product Liability Insurance You Carry:		
Comments:		

The more information you can supply, the better. Photographs and product brochures or specification sheets are helpful.

The Purchase Order Demystified

A *purchase order* is a document authorizing the buying of a product or service. It is a legal contract and its terms must be followed precisely to be honored. Familiarize yourself with purchase orders before initiating a relationship with home shopping channels.

Sometimes a purchase order, often called the *P.O.*, is simple. Sometimes it is almost unintelligible.

A typical P.O. contains the following information:

1. Name, address and phone number of purchaser
2. Date, payment terms, freight terms and P.O. number
3. FOB (origin of product), ship via_____
4. Do not ship before the date _____or after the date _____
5. Your name, billing address and ship-to address
6. Their item number and the number assigned to the product by the station
7. Quantity ordered, product type, unit cost and total cost
8. Special instructions
9. Signed by or authorization

A purchase order is usually subject to conditions that are written—most often in small print. Always read it thoroughly and if you have *any* questions, ask.

The typical sequence of events from initiation of purchase order through order placement is shown in Figure 2.9.

FIGURE 2.9
Purchase Order Flow

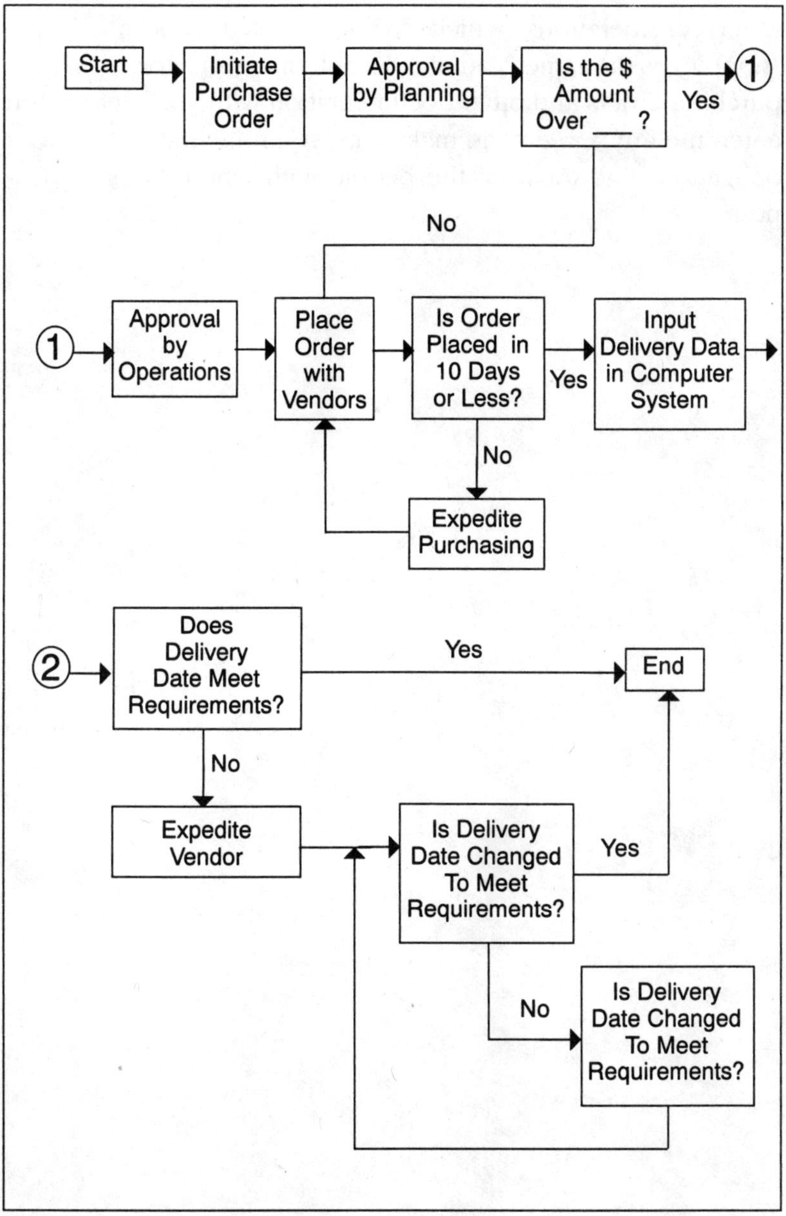

Legal Consultation

Many new enterprises involve new forms, paperwork and other considerations, which you may not understand. Home shopping is the same. You may want to have an attorney review purchase orders and other documentation with you. Before you enter into any agreement, make sure you fully understand your obligations and those of the people with whom you do business.

☑ Preparing To Submit Your Product—Checklist

This checklist is designed to assist in preparing to submit your product.

- ☐ 1. Research the right station(s) for your product.
- ☐ 2. Price your product.
- ☐ 3. Create a persuasive product presentation.
- ☐ 4. Consult legal counsel in regard to protecting your product (via patent and/or trademark), and also to clarify forms, documents, purchase orders.
- ☐ 5. Contact insurance companies to lay the groundwork for a $1 million product liability policy.

CHAPTER 3

Selling a Home Shopping Channel on Your Product

Your Step-by-Step Outline To Sell a Station

Each home shopping channel has different guidelines for product submission. Submitting to smaller stations may be as easy as calling first, then sending off the sample. The larger channels require that you fill out a questionnaire before you submit. If they are interested, they will then request a sample. Then you will send the sample in UPS-approved packaging, generic or otherwise.

Here are the 11 steps:

1. Call each station and find out what their guidelines are for the submission of a product. The larger stations usually route you to a person or recorder where you

leave your name and address. They will send you a questionnaire together with their procedures for product submission.

2. Unless absolutely necessary, do not call your buyer on Monday mornings or on their meeting days. It is best to communicate in the later part of the week, if possible. If you can't reach your buyer, there is a reason. Find out that reason. Is it periodic meetings? Maybe they don't like calls during this time period. Again, keep notes on this.
3. Most stations are in the Eastern time zone. If you live in the West, station buyers may be putting telephone calls through to you prior to 9:00 A.M. Make sure you are there! As convenient as voice mail, answering machines and beepers are, they will be of little use to you if you have to try to make a return phone call to busy buyers. Answer that phone!
4. Persist. You may have to call frequently, varying the times of day you call to reach the buyer.
5. Use your fax persistently, too. At times it is easier to communicate via fax, since the buyer will eventually read it.
6. When you have made contact and have the guidelines, ship your product.
7. Call three weeks after the buyer has received the product to see if there is initial interest. To reinforce your presence, fax that same day asking the same thing if you've had to leave a message, which is usually the case.
8. Follow up every tenth business day, both via phone and fax until you actually connect with the station buyer.
9. Once you have reached the buyer, let him or her talk. Let them explain their interest or concerns without becoming defensive. Ask about the buyer's schedule.

When is the best time to call? Write down which days are meeting days and make a note not to telephone the buyer then.

10. If your product is declined, you will be informed by letter or a call.
11. If your product is accepted, your station buyer will keep you informed as to everything that will transpire from this point on.

As this step-by-step outline indicates, *persistence is pivotal to accomplishing your goal. Don't let bad timing and delays undermine your objectives. The customer needs your product!*

Taking Advantage of Open-Buy Days

Some stations, especially the larger ones, have an acquisition policy called "open-buy days." This means you set an appointment with a buyer for a specific time and then get 15 minutes or less to show your product. This is a terrific way to present your product personally. However, you will have to travel. If the cost is not prohibitive, ask the station if they have open-buy days, then make an appointment.

The open-buy day can take place at any time in the wooing process. It might be your first contact with the station buyer; or it might occur after you've submitted.

Submitting Your Product

First impressions are everything, especially in a competitive market such as home shopping. Every part of the submission process will count either in your favor or against you. Therefore, I am giving you a few points to consider when submitting your product:

1. Each aspect of your submission should be perfect—the paperwork, the product and the packaging.
2. Check the product yourself. Make sure there are no flaws.
3. Is it securely packed in its container? The way you send your product to station buyers is the way they will want it sent to the customer (pending approval).
4. Printing on your brochures or instructions should include only your name, address and phone number. For example:

   For additional or replacement parts, contact:
   ABC Company
   123 USA Street
   Anywhere, USA 00011
   800-123-1111

5. Anything soliciting more than this will probably be rejected by the station's quality assurance. As a rule, stations do not allow instructions or brochures in the packaging that solicit any additional sales except replacement parts. However, you may be able to negotiate the inclusion of such material with the station buyer. Talk over with him or her the possibility of soliciting further sales or possibly inserting your own catalog if you have related products.

Selling the Buyer in Writing—Don't Get Lost in the Pile

1. Explain why you believe that the buyer you are addressing will be interested in your product.

2. Be specific about your product. Create a catchy title or subtitles about your product to convey its essence.
3. Describe your product's main points. Illustrations are helpful.
4. Show how your product is fresh and different from comparable products. Also, tell how it fulfills needs for the general public that no other product has yet filled.
5. Convey your enthusiasm about your product. Enthusiasm is contagious; buyers are more inclined to be attracted to a product that comes surrounded by strong convictions.
6. If you are available and want to present your product with the host, let the buyer know that this is an option.
7. Send any documentation to the buyer concerning the product that may be helpful, including testimonial letters from customers who have already used it.

Keeping Quality Assurance Uppermost

When the station receives your submission, it will be thoroughly analyzed by quality assurance.

All stations have quality assurance programs. Your product must stand on its own in this division. They test the product to make sure it is sound and conforms to their standards. They also verify that the product meets claims made in any brochures or accompanying instructions. If there are specified parts, are they as indicated in the written description? For example, if it says "10 ft. electrical cord," the cord must be 10 feet long, period. No exceptions.

The buyer is not concerned about the packaging as long as it is UPS approved and conforms to their standards. It is the contents that they are interested in, since that is what will air on their program. Nonetheless, *if the packaging or product is rejected by quality assurance, it may set you back 90 days or keep you off the air completely. Packaging is very important.* It must meet UPS specifications. If you already have retail packaging completed, it must qualify to be shipped "as is" through UPS too. If not, get a standard generic box that conforms to UPS shipping regulations as a master carton. Small quantities may be purchased at your local box or shipping retailer.

To illustrate how important the appropriate shipping is, let me recount my own experience. I submitted a small product in retail packaging that could be folded square and passed UPS standards. The package could also be folded to hang from a pegboard in a store as a point-of-purchase display. Quality assurance did not approve this very expensive packaging. There was concern that it would snag on UPS conveyor belts. After a delay, we resubmitted in a square generic white box and it was accepted.

Selling a Home Shopping Channel on Your Product—Checklist

- ☐ 1. Obtain submission guidelines from the station.
- ☐ 2. Fill out submission forms and return to station buyer.
- ☐ 3. Send product sample.
- ☐ 4. Analyze product unit cost and suggested retail price and confirm with station.
- ☐ 5. Find out the best times and ways to contact your station buyer.
- ☐ 6. Make sure communication paths are set up (call forwarding and call waiting) so you *never* miss a call from the buyer.
- ☐ 7. When faxing, keep the message brief and to the point so it is easy to read. I always hand-write these. It makes it more personal and catches the buyer's eye.
- ☐ 8. Keep a daily calendar for the next possible date and times when you should contact the station buyer.

CHAPTER

4

Closing the Deal

Following Up with the Station Buyer

Just like most of us, station buyers are extremely busy people. Knowing this, you may be intimidated about asking questions. You may feel that admitting to ignorance is a sign of weakness. You may also be reluctant to risk ridicule by asking questions.

Moreover, it's assumed that mastery in anything makes that field the exclusive territory of specialists. You may be afraid to ask questions because you take for granted that the information you'll receive will be unintelligible anyway.

Assumptions aside, you need to understand the way the station operates if you are going to do business with it. The insights that follow are not intended to replace information you will get from station buyers. However, the description of the way stations work is in lay terms. You'll discover easy ways to access information and can develop effective processing strategies suited to your particular situation.

Viewers will buy *benefits*, those features of your product that make it outstanding. Therefore, so does the station buyer. The buyer will be looking for aspects of your product that will make it irresistible to the viewing audience. When you are ready to contact the station buyer, have a list in front of you that fully outlines the benefits of your product, both to the station and to the consumer. This will help him or her build a mental picture of how the product can be directed to the viewer.

Making the Deal

Deal-making is an art, and you may not acquire finesse overnight. Real deal-makers most often cultivated their skills over a long period and with much practice. Like many arts, deal-making expertise is measurably dependent on knowledge. You have to know what is negotiable and what is not. The vendor's bargaining chip is some flexibility in the price. For your first sale to a station, the station's only bargaining chip may be their payment plan. Once you have done some business with a station, you may be able to negotiate for a better time slot during which your product airs.

I use the following metaphor not to condone hunting or guns, but rather to illustrate an attitude that is very important in sales. I grew up on a farm in Iowa, and we hunted for food. This may sound like a stretch, but I really feel that the hunting experience has helped make me into a good salesperson. Think of it: We call a hunter a *hunter* because 99% of what he or she does is *hunt*. The hunter is not called a *killer* because of the kill. That is the end product of the hunt. When working with a buyer, you should be like a hunter. If one sales approach falls flat, try another. Everything you do must be leading to an eventual sale, leading to a situation that tantalizes the buyer with an offer he or she cannot refuse. Your "kill" is the sale.

At all times, make sure to hunt with a loaded gun. It is useless to hunt without real ammunition. This means reading all up-to-date articles on home shopping, comparable products and the specific company you are pursuing. Know the trends. This will assure you and your buyer that you are professional, that your guns are not loaded with blanks.

Pulling Out All the Stops To Counter Buyer Objections

Automatic responses can kill deals before they even get off the ground. Buyers regularly refuse new products. Countless other potentially great products never see the light of day just because vendors are too easily cowed by rejection. If you do not want to have your product squelched by your buyer, you must learn to identify and confront common rejection phrases when you hear them. Here are some examples:

Rejection	**Response**
"Your product does not fit our philosophy."	Easily explain why your product requires change in philosophy, a "paradigm shift." Also point out the consequences of ignoring this shift. Speak of innovation.
"Your product will be turned down in our sales committee meeting."	Ask: "How can we modify the sales presentation so they will see how exceptional my product is?" Admit you do not have all the answers and you need the buyer's input. Listen and respond.

"Products in this category have not done well in the past."	Say, "Times are changing. Today is different and this product has different qualities such as . . . (cost, improved, broader appeal, etc.)."

If your targeted station buyer expresses reservations by letter, use the same kind of persuasive responses. A typical rejection letter from a station buyer is brief and impersonal. It reads something like this:

> Dear Sir/Madam:
>
> Unfortunately we regret that we cannot accept your product at this time. It does not fit our current trend. We wish you the best of luck.
>
> Sincerely,
>
> (name of station buyer)

I recommend what might be considered a "loaded gun" response, such as that shown in Figure 4.1. See how you can make your offer tough to refuse. Tap every angle you can think of and use layers of persuasion that include lower prices, etc.

Getting Paid: Stations' Payment Plans

Naturally, one of your major considerations will be payment. Cash flow and risk are two very important factors to consider, the more so for small businesses and one-person operators.

Typically, stations have one of the following purchasing options:

FIGURE 4.1
One Response to a Station Buyer's Rejection

Dear (name of station buyer):

With great interest, I recently read a newspaper article about your company. It mentioned that you are looking for basic product appealing to your customer base. In addition, I understand that you are doing a 50-state tour, looking for new product.

I noticed that one of the products on your station is similar to mine. I would like to point out a couple of additional benefits that my product offers: One, the quality of our raw materials is better than the competition's. And two, our price point looks as if it might be less.

I would like to talk with you about getting this on your channel, since the other product did quite well on your state-to-state tours.

I have also gone back to my suppliers to see if I could get an additional discount. Much to my satisfaction, I did. This again lowers my cost to you. $$$$.

Let's reopen dialogue on this product. In the very near future, I would be free to meet with you on an open-buy day if you wish.

Please reconsider this product.

Sincerely,

- *30-day net*: You will be paid approximately 30 days from the time they receive your product.
- *60-day net*: You will be paid approximately 60 days from the time they receive your product.

- *90-day net*: You will be paid approximately 90 days from the time they receive your product.
- *Guaranteed sale*: You are paid 30 days after receipt of the product, only if it sells. The station has the option of returning unsold items or doing another show. There are risks to consider with this plan, so do not send too much product for the first show.
- *Advanced purchase*: The station sells the product before they receive it. (This is very rare.) Here, the vendor is paid for exactly what the buyer orders.

Liability narrows with 30-, 60- or 90-day net payment plans. However, the more risky guaranteed sales are the trend. This is the way QVC and others do business. If negotiations are possible, make sure the payment situation fits you and your company. Most often negotiations are minimal, since you have already filled in your best price for a volume order on the submission forms.

Negotiating for a Better Airtime

Keep in mind that buyers have to fill 24 hours' worth of programming time, seven days a week. You may have to negotiate for better programming time.

Sales are best in the hours you might expect—from 3 P.M. to 11 P.M. Days of the week are also significant. In my experience, sales on holiday weekends are about half that of normal days. Some weekends are better than weekdays, but this is not always true. It depends on what programming other channels have scheduled. There may be national events such as the Super Bowl with which your airing will compete.

If you happen to get a poor programming slot, negotiate for a better one the second time around.

Communicating with Your Scheduled Host

The more the program host knows about your product, the better presentation he or she will be able to make while on air. Prior to airtime, you should convey as much information to the host as you can, most often through the buyer. You may also be able to talk to the host by telephone and relay information through brochures, manuals and videotapes. You may want to send the host a sample product to use. This enables him or her to give actual testimony as to its use and effectiveness. *A point of protocol*: Do not communicate with the host without first asking the buyer. Some of the larger stations have secretaries for their host; you may be able to communicate through them.

Listening In on a Real Conversation with a Home Shopping Buyer

To sum up how stations work, I have included this sample conversation. On April 29, 1994, I was speaking with Jennifer Yeager, then station buyer and hostess at Future Mart, a home shopping station in the New York area, now at VIA-TV in Knoxville, Tennessee. This should give you added insight on the station buyer/host perspective.

Q: What is your position?
A: I am the show hostess and product manager.

Q: What are your responsibilities as a product manager?
A: I select products. I choose which products go on the air, figure which products go to which show. I request a sample and have the vendor (you) fill out a product information form.

Q: What types of classifications are you looking for at present?
A: At this point, we are growing so rapidly that we have been looking at a broad spectrum of merchandise.

Q: Packaging: Do you prefer it in retail or generic or does it matter?
A: Generally, it does not matter.

Q: First you mentioned that you have the vendors submit a questionnaire. At what point, if a vendor calls you, do you want to see an actual sample?
A: Initially, if someone calls and is soliciting business—I get many of these calls a day—most of the time it is merchandise I cannot use. Usually, by my initial phone call I have a very good feeling if it is viable for us or not. I'll tell all of them to send me some literature or any written information even if I think it is something we cannot use. I may be wrong with my first impression.

Q: Let's say you get the literature and the product looks like it is something you want to do. Do you then have them send a sample?
A: Yes.

Q: Okay. Based on the sample, you now like it. What transpires from that point?
A: They fill out a product information sheet. I need to know how many they have in stock. I ask if there are any videotapes on the product. Because we may incorporate video for our show, this is very important.

Q: When you say "numbers in stock," that would vary according to the product, right?
A: Yes.

Q: Do you have open-buy days?
A: No.

Q: Do you do seasonal products?
A: Absolutely.

Q: Such as Father's Day, Mother's Day...?
A: Yes, very important.

Q: What hours do you consider the best for putting a product on air?
A: Prime time evening.

Q: We have four time zones, so?
A: We try to cover all four of them.

Q: So you would rotate the product through the time zones?
A: Yes.

Q: What hours do you air there presently?
A: Running 24 hours, at first we weren't, but now we are.

Q: What product surprised you the most? You thought it was going to do okay, but it did exceptionally well. You don't have to be specific, just the category.
A: Let's see. Something that just happened recently, let me refresh my memory. I was showing some jewelry on the air, beautiful, beautiful rings and tennis bracelets. Incorporated into the presentation, however, were some, in my opinion, unappealing pendants. They flew out the door. Granted, they were $5 to $10 cheaper than the rings.

Q: So the pendants took off like mad?
A: I was surprised about that. When I was setting up for the show I was saying, they are okay, but they're a filler. I didn't think they'd do that well. But they did.

Q: Again, on the same line, what product surprised you because you thought it was going to do very well and didn't? Again, it's okay to be general.
A: We had a palm-size computer. I do not want to name names, but I thought it was the best on the market and

considering we were cheaper than anyone else, it was certainly worth the value. I was expecting it to fly out of here. It just did adequately. You really have to demonstrate and have the right sales pitch. Because if you do it properly and the product is good, it will sell. If it doesn't sell, you are doing something wrong with your sales approach.

Q: This question might be repetitive. If I call you for the first time and had a new product, are there any "top three" questions or things you want to know about the product right away?
A: How much for wholesale? Profit margin? And what is it? And numbers in stock?

Q: Do you do close-outs? (When a company decides not to manufacture any more and maybe have 10,000 on hand that they would like to unload.)
A: Absolutely.

Q: Jennifer, I'd like to quickly move to your responsibilities as a hostess. How many years have you been a hostess with Future Mart?
A: One year with Future Mart. I worked for other shopping networks prior to Future Mart.

Q: Why were you interested in getting into this business or did it just happen? Did you aggressively apply for this position?
A: No. It just happened. I've done TV commercials and taken acting lessons in the past, and I also worked in the field for a fashion designer as a sales manager. The combination of the studying acting and a strong background in sales, those two experiences led to this.

Q: So you transitioned into it and being at the right place at the right time for the station?
A: Yes.

Q: You've already mentioned that you had tremendous growth in the last year. Over all, not just talking about Future Mart, but with your experience and where you've been, how do you foresee the growth of home shopping in the future?
A: It *is* the future!

Q: I like that.
A: I'll tell you, when I started working at the other shopping channels a few years ago, I'd call people and they would say they did not want their product on a home shopping channel. I had a hard time talking to people and getting a quality product on the program. Now, two and a half years later, I am bombarded with people faxing and calling—"Please, please put my product on your show." The attitude has changed completely, 100 percent.

Q: What shows do you enjoy doing the most? When I say "shows," maybe what types of product.
A: Oh, it varies. I do not know. I do not like selling the same product over and over again. I enjoy different products. I like to interact with the audience—I love that. It's very important. The call-ins. Again, going back to a previous question, it is very important that the audience know the product so if it needs to be demonstrated, a TV-quality video is very important, so they can understand what it does.

Q: How long do you run an average product? I mean is it 5 minutes, 10 minutes, 15 minutes?
A: Well, the higher the price of the product, the longer we would spend on it. If it is a $15 product, we might spend ten minutes. If it is a $1,500 product, we could spend as much as a half hour on it.

Q: Okay now, what if, let's say, it takes the audience two, three or four minutes to catch onto what it [a product] is.

You might need a demo. Do you give the product ample time, or do you consider that when choosing the product?
A: I guess I would consider that when choosing the product.

Q: So, in other words, it would have to have a little more time because it is not going to sell itself?
A: You could put the greatest product up there, but if you do not have the right sales approach or time, it won't sell. Most products need to be "sold." However, rarely you could just sit there and say nothing and the phones will ring off the hook.

Q: Do you have plans for doing the longer type shows like infomercials?
A: Sure. I think shopping channels and infomercials are combining themselves, like QVC started infomercials through other channels and Value Vision is now getting into infomercials.

Q: You mentioned that your callers call in and you enjoy that. Do you anticipate more talk show–style shows in the future?
A: We will do about the same.

Q: More and more stations are getting in home shopping. With the information superhighway, people are able to shop through their computers. Specialization, in other words. Might stations get more specialized into the category of the products they are selling?
A: Absolutely, with specialty shopping channels.

Q: Are there any advantages I would have to calling Future Mart over another station? Let's say, automatically, that you were going to take my product.
A: One of the advantages is that we are an informative shopping channel. That is why we ask for a tape if they

have one. We *inform* our viewers of the product; we don't just put a product up there. Even if something is bad about a product, we'll say it: "It has been known to do this, but it is a good investment." We tell the truth, we'll show them how to use it, we educate them. We just don't say, "Here is a gemstone." We tell them to look in the catalog, how to mount its setting. We tell them what type of opal it is, its hardness, quality, retail value, the whole process, everything they want to know. We are an educational shopping channel.

Q: Thanks for your time, Jennifer. Good luck at VIA-TV.

To be an entrepreneur requires much, much more than having a great idea. You have got to have the initiative, drive and ingenuity to push that great idea into the marketplace. Part of covering all your bases is presenting your product in the best possible light. This does not necessarily mean a long letter or a barrage of jargon. By keeping your presentation as simple as possible, you raise the chances of your buyer absorbing your message. However, if the documentation will sway him or her, by all means send it.

The buyer's ultimate responsibility is to the station's customers. They are the end judge. If the buyer has chosen good products, they will sell.

Closing the Deal—Checklist

- ☐ 1. Send product documentation and advertising claim substantiation to station.
- ☐ 2. Send existing public relations material on product to station's buyer.
- ☐ 3. Send existing film, video and still photographs of product to station's buyer.
- ☐ 4. Follow up with station's buyer as many times as required.
- ☐ 5. Consult with show host where possible after closing.

CHAPTER
5

Getting Your Product Ready for Post-Show Success

Getting It Done: Manufacturing, Assembly and Packaging

If you are an individual, inventor or small business and do not want to embroil your household in a cottage industry, there are many other ways to set up the manufacturing process.

Your product category, materials and components are going to dictate the companies that you need to contact. There are thousands of manufacturers for all types of products. You may find resources simply by looking through your local yellow pages. The library has directories of manufacturers and their classifications such as the *Thomas Register of American Manufacturers*.

Once you have found several leads, narrow your options by telephoning and visiting their operations if necessary. Make sure they are going to be there when you need them. Look at where they are working: Do they look stable? Submit your specifications for quotations. Once you have received quotations, check out the companies with which you have decided to contract. Ask for references, banking information (average balance, how long have they banked there, have they ever bounced checks, etc.) and a Dun & Bradstreet Report.

Confirm that the companies have not only the right price, but also the ability to deliver a *quality* product *on time.* Otherwise, all is for naught. Also locate a second manufacturer that could produce the component if the first option falls through.

If your product requires only assembly, a fulfillment house may be all you need. Small manufacturers in your area will be able to guide you to local operations that do this type of work.

Your manufacturer may be able to package your product or direct you to an outfit that can. If not, you can find a packager through the yellow pages.

You can use the clout that surrounds home shopping sales to control your cash flow. On the purchase order, arrange to pay the companies that supply you when you receive payment from the station. You will be amazed to find that most manufacturers will work with you this way.

The following flowcharts illustrate how the home shopping revolution puts marketing power back in the hands of individuals. In the past, the entrepreneur or inventor had a tough time getting through the maze from idea to retail. Now, thanks to home shopping, an individual can get the prototype to the buyer in idea form only. If the buyer shows interest, this individual can proceed directly to manufacturing, securing credit with a supplier based on the purchase order from the station. It is like going from *A* directly to *Z*, and in the process saving considerable money, time and labor. This will work only with products for which the manufacturing time is short.

Old Order

Idea ➔ Prototype ➔ Manufacture ➔ Warehouse ➔ Sell ➔ Ship ➔ Retail ➔ End Sale

New Order

Idea ➔ Prototype ➔ Sell ➔ Manufacture ➔ Warehouse ➔ Ship ➔ Retail ➔ End Sale

Credit is set up immediately at the "sell" point and is tied to the purchase order.

Shipping

Shipping can be very easy as long as there is communication between you and your workers, as well as you and your buyer and shipping personnel at the station. Make sure all parties involved understand all phases.

Shipping instructions (SIs) come in many forms, from simple to complex. The larger stations will send you a manual with all of their requirements. Read them carefully and communicate with all concerned. You may be fined if you do not follow all guidelines precisely.

Packaging will usually take place at your factory, fulfillment house or warehouse. If your order is large, you may want to check it out yourself prior to loading. Do not overlook details such as stamping the purchaser's item number on each box and marking each skid with the total number of items and number of master cartons.

Some smaller stations may want you to drop-ship directly to the customers who have ordered your product. One advantage of this method is that usually items are shipped in a staggered fashion, rather than all at once. However, it is more costly. Remember this when pricing your product.

The station will send you labels of all the customers who have ordered your product. Simply address the shipping packages and out they go.

Putting It All Together

To help you see how to physically get the manufacturing done, let's take a look at the manufacturing plan I developed for a product called the "Portable Line Drive," a manual baseball-softball pitching machine.

First, I broke the product down into its various components—the smallest denominators—to determine what kind of manufacturing I needed. The breakdown is outlined in the project plan (Figure 5.1). The next step was contacting the manufacturers of these various parts, always investigating for price, quality and on-time delivery.

Bat ➔ Cut Groove

The bat was the most expensive part of my product. Therefore, it was important to get a competitive price for it. To source bat manufacturers, I went to two local sporting goods stores and copied names and addresses off the bats. I called every major bat manufacturer in the U.S. The variance in prices and also the enthusiasm for helping my company surprised me. After analyzing all the input (price, quality, delivery policy, terms), I picked a national bat manufacturer.

I traveled to their factory to make sure they understood what I needed and the importance of scheduling to meet the home shopping market. They convinced me that they could meet my

FIGURE 5.1
Project Plan

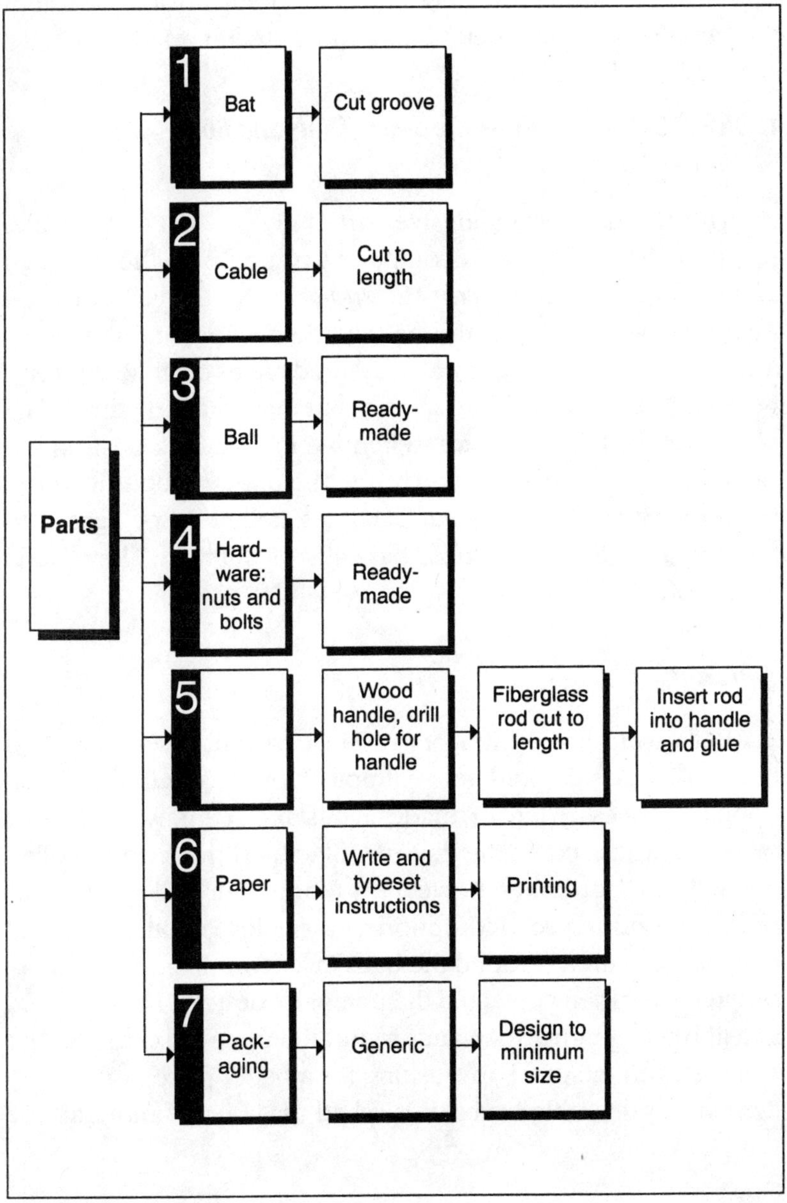

requirements at an agreeable price. They also agreed to cut a groove in my bats (part of the design, but a separate element). Although this was another denominator, doing business through the same supplier built clout and eliminated an extra step.

Cable ➔ Cut to Length ➔ Hardware (Nuts and Bolts) ➔ Ready-Made

The second most expensive part of my product was a cable. Again I called every cable company I could find either through *Thomas Register of American Manufacturers* or the yellow pages. Again, I was amazed at the wide variety in pricing as well as interest in my project. They also assured me of on-time delivery.

I honed my search further to a national company that had a plant about 100 miles away. When we had made a deal on the cable, I asked them about hardware, the nuts and bolts it would require to hook the whole apparatus together. They agreed to furnish all at a terrific price, basically as a favor. They made their money in cable.

Ball ➔ Ready-Made

Balls were not a third priority in cost, but it was essential that I made sure I could get an ample supply early in the development process. Here, I made a mistake. I knew a national sales rep with a company that manufactured the kind of balls I needed. After ordering, however, I found their ball quality was poor. I found my second option in a catalog, another national ball manufacturer. (I found the balls in a sporting goods catalog, ordered one, then contacted the company directly.) I negotiated a deal by telephone, then later found the price to be too high. I went back to the company, asking for a better price point. They agreed to preferable terms, but asked that I order more at one time. I did, but I had them deliver the balls over a period of time rather than all at once. We both won.

Pitch Stick ➔ Wood Handle, Drill Hole for Handle ➔ Fiberglass Rod Cut to Length ➔ Insert Rod into Handle and Glue

Since I already had so much cooperation from other suppliers, composing a manufacturing scheme for the Portable Line Drive was turning out to be more of a snap than I had anticipated. The pitch stick was my fourth order of business. Since the handle was wood and I was buying from a wood bat manufacturer, I called to see if they knew a company that could make the wood dowel (handle) for me. They did! They referred me to another company. Thus, I found the manufacturer of that element too.

The fiberglass rod element was not so simple. I had to go back to the *Thomas Register of American Manufacturers* to flush out a manufacturer from scratch. Finally, after 20 calls, I contracted for a great price.

Paper ➔ Compose and Typeset Instructions ➔ Printing

The typesetting and printing business has changed dramatically in the past few years. I was able to typeset my instructions and labels using a computer in my neighborhood (since I did not have one then). I then took the artwork to my local quick-print shop. The prices at these operations are fantastic unless you are doing a run of more than 100,000.

Packaging ➔ Generic ➔ Design to Minimum Size

There are many box manufacturers. Unless you are going to order 50,000 to 100,000, I've found it is best to buy a standard generic box from a manufacturer in a major city near you. Most have them. I found mine in the *Thomas Register of American Manufacturers*. I looked for the smallest possible size. A small, full box is safer and more economical to ship, making your price more competitive.

Final Assembly

With all the suppliers lined up, the only remaining assembly was cutting my cable to the desired length, assembling the pitch stick and doing the packaging. Initially, we bought the necessary tools, then rented space to assemble and package everything. Later we farmed this final assembly out to a fulfillment house.

This turned out to be a fantastic plan for the product and we were able to deliver large numbers in a short period of time. All went well! My product was essentially a low tech one, not requiring any molding or electronics. Do not be daunted by either process. Again, the key is finding the right people to supply your parts. I have had molds made in Taiwan and electronics made in Southern California.

It is interesting where your sourcing leads you. This search is an adventure in and of itself, part of the "hunt."

Getting Your Product Ready for Post-Show Success—Checklist

- ☐ 1. Break the product down into its smallest common denominators, as many pieces as practically possible.
- ☐ 2. Call as many suppliers as you can to get the right mix of capability and cost, terms and delivery for each part of the manufacturing process.
- ☐ 3. However, buy as many parts from as few suppliers as possible, increasing your clout with each one.
- ☐ 4. Your manufacturing goal should always be "funneled" this way, that is, start with a broad number of aspects and hone them down into a narrow range of suppliers.

CHAPTER
6

After You Are on the Air—Post-Show Analysis

Record and Review Your Segment

When your program segment airs, make sure to videotape the showing of your product. The stations will help you with this since they have VCRs right there. You can use this copy to analyze the effectiveness of both the station and your material.

Look at any mistakes you may have made. Look at any mistakes the station may have made. See where the presentation or the product could be improved. Did it look and sound the best it could?

Communicate any needed changes to the station buyer. Be diplomatic in this communication, commenting on the positives and encouraging the station to spend more airtime on those. If the show goes well, leave it alone.

My Own Pre-Show Orientation

I was lucky my first time on QVC. First, I got a great hostess, Mary Beth Roe. We spent about 20 minutes prior to airtime going over the product. Roe also wanted some personal information about me, to make the demonstration go smoother.

It is a total thrill to go on air. The host will try to keep you calm. Although I had been selling throughout my adult life, I was very keyed up and nervous. There are a ton of lights, cameras and people behind the screens. They quickly taught me which camera to look at, and it was *showtime*!

Just before the show, I learned that there was a digital counter facing the hostess and me. This counter indicated exactly what sold while I was on stage. The opening included the usual introductions—myself, the models demonstrating the product and most importantly, the product itself. Typically, you get 7.5 to 8 minutes per product. This may vary with the type of product and type of show. We were selling two products at once, the Portable Line Drive and Youth Line Drive for kids. Since we had two products, we got a 15-minute show.

On the Air

Mary Beth Roe held the show together by asking questions of me and very clearly describing the products, with emphasis on quality. If conversation drifted, she immediately pulled the focus back to the products and their benefits. QVC offered the Portable Line Drive for $37.75 + shipping and the Youth Line Drive for $19.95 + shipping.

At the time, I did not know that she, like all hosts, had a microphone in her ear. The producer/director talks to hosts most of the time, relaying sales info, show info and any relevant issues that may help the sales. This is incredible to me. Can you talk and listen at the same time? This is central to their job.

It was like being on another planet. Had I not taped the show, I would not have remembered anything. The time flew by. In the middle of the show, I got a boost of confidence when I saw, on the digital read out, that we had sold about half of our first sale to QVC. It was like being resuscitated.

The digital meter kept advancing forward at an incredible rate—900 units sold, 1,000, 1,150, 1,300. Callers had purchased 1,500 Portable Line Drives and 500 Youth Line Drives for the first show! Then came the biggest surprise of all—the "green room."

The Green Room

The green room was a comfortable place just offstage decorated much the same as anyone's living room. There I was offered snacks and beverages and ran into stars Morgan Fairchild and Phyllis George. The room was flanked with computers, and a television aired the live presentation that followed mine. The computers gave me a complete financial analysis of my products' performance. The numbers were being updated by the second. The show hadn't been over two minutes and we had sold 70 percent of our inventory. This meant I had sold more product in 17 minutes than I had in the previous 45 days.

The computer readings included the following:

- Number of units sold
- Dollar volume sold
- Customers buying multiple units
- Number of people on hold talking to the people that take orders

- Number of people ordering electronically, by entering charge numbers and other indicators on their push-button phones

A quick analysis showed that just five minutes after the show 1,500 had sold, 400 callers were on hold or ordering and 50 were buying electronically. Added up, we were just 50 short of our 2,000 inventory. We had almost sold out when I left the green room.

In this brief interlude following our show, I was able to make a reasonable analysis of both the presentation and the efficacy of the home shopping venue. We had sold to QVC at a fair profit. Now, it was clear that the channel would return none of that product.

QVC measures a good show at $2,000 worth of sales per minute. Our product sold over $4,000 per minute! The QVC people labeled the show a mega-hit. This ensured another order. The next day, we received an order for 3,000 units to show again in four weeks.

It does not take a genius to figure out that this type of exposure gives you unheard-of advertising while making a substantial income.

Projections and Communications

The real post-show analysis began when I spoke with the buyer about second orders. QVC gave us our second order one day after the first show. That gave me only two and a half weeks to get it ready, but that was enough. This post-show conversation with the buyer could not have been more critical, because I was working with on-time delivery. We also needed to talk about what would transpire if show number two were a sellout. If that happened, she said she would probably order more units and air show numbers three and four; however, she did not commit to any exact numbers.

At that point, I had to get my pencil sharpened and start projecting, conservatively as well as optimistically. I contacted my vendors to make sure they would have ample stock on hand for more orders. We decided to order enough from our vendors to cover middle ground. (Our conservative estimate of sales was 4,000 units. Our optimistic projection was 8,000. We ordered 6,000.)

Having alerted my vendors, I had an idea of how much lead time I would need in case I needed more units. I could communicate this scheduling to the buyer.

In our case, we wanted to make sure we could provide the buyer with as many units as they desired. This is not always necessary. You may have a set limit, a maximum that you provide per month. The buyer can work within those constraints.

Your primary concern is that you do not end up with an excessive inventory when your show ends.

CHAPTER 7

Fitting Infomercials into the Mix

What Is an Infomercial?

An infomercial is a 28-minute segment of TV time that is actually a sales presentation of a particular product disguised as a show. The vendor buys this time slot from the station to showcase the product. There are usually two to three opportunities in that time segment for the viewer to go to the phone and purchase whatever the product is. This is why the term "direct response" also describes infomercials.

Infomercials may prove one of the most dynamic marketing techniques in years to come. Here's why:

1. They cut the cost of media exposure by as much as 75 percent.
2. Huge TV exposure drives retail sales.

3. The half-hour gives you the ability to fully explain your product's benefits directly to a large potential customer base.
4. You get on-the-spot results so you can determine whether your product will generate profits. People call in and order immediately. They do not order later. They order now.
5. Even as a small company, you can break into the same market as larger companies.
6. Your customer list has a value all its own for accessories and future products. In addition, you can sell the customer list to other companies for anywhere from $.04 to a $1.00 a name.

Many times entrepreneurs wonder whether they must be successful with a short shopping channel segment on TV before they consider an infomercial. From personal experience, I discovered that a product that has done well on an infomercial will almost always do well on home shopping. However, the converse is not true. A product that sells well on home shopping does not necessarily thrive when shown as an infomercial.

Certainly, more infomercials are made than air on television. Some sources estimate that one out of 100 actually makes it to the viewer. And an even lower percentage of those that air perform well.

To help you gauge your product's suitability for the infomercial market, here are rates of viewer motivation to buy given attributes:

Quality	88%	Endorsement	42%
Technology	48	Mainstream	57
Urgency	76	Self-Improvement	90
Scarcity	73	Well-Being	74
Uniqueness	79	Ambitions	67
Attractiveness	84	Money Back	96

If you are considering an infomercial, you must bear in mind the following:

- Mass appeal is a must. Does your product have it?
- Infomercials are costly, not only to make but to air.
- The risk is greater but the potential returns are, too.

A Comparison of Infomercials Versus Home Shopping

The major differences between selling via an infomercial and home shopping are many; however, the following are key:

Infomercial	Home Shopping
You take all the risk	Home shopping channel shares the risk
You sell retail	You sell wholesale
Huge investment	Investment in product only
Lengthy time investment	Short time investment
Possible huge return	Possible moderate return

Viewer Response to a TV Message

It's easy to see that infomercials may not be as captivating as we would all like them to be. When commercials interrupt whatever show viewers are actually watching, 38 percent grab their remote and change the channel, 22 percent slip off to the bathroom, 18 percent forage in the kitchen and only 15 percent actually watch the commercial. The remaining 6 percent are doing something else. We hope it is running off to the telephone to call the 1(800) number they heard previously, but probably not.

Repetition prevails upon this 6 percent. Few viewers actually sit there poised with pencil in hand waiting to buy. At first, the viewer is going to perceive the product as, at best, a "whatyamajigger." By the end of the second viewing, there is usually a vague understanding of what is going on. By the third exposure, the viewer "gets it." It may take three airings of the infomercial before the viewer finally figures out that he or she needs that item. The purchase impact of a repeated infomercial in direct response is as follows in sales per spot:

Category	First Time Aired	Second Time Aired
Automobile	5.0	7.2
Exercise	2.5	6.4
Music	2.4	4.5
Coins	3.4	4.4
Hair	3.2	4.3
Pet	2.6	3.8
Water	3.0	3.2
Knife	1.6	2.6

Most infomercials play in two or three parts to compensate for these incremental understanding levels. Often, they will repeat themselves two or three times, slightly modifying each demonstration. This has been demonstrated to be the most effective way to spur the viewer to buy.

Creating an Infomercial

I have found that the best way to create an infomercial is through an infomercial production company. Although the idea of creating the segment yourself may at first sound appealing, the truth is that an infomercial production company will likely be able to do a better job for less money. Moreover, they sometimes purchase blocks of time on channels that run infomercials or they can refer you to a broker who will secure time for you. As such, they can help you through the system.

Begin by contacting the National Infomercial Marketing Association (NIMA):

NIMA
1201 New York Avenue, N.W., Suite 1000
Washington, DC 20005
Phone: 202-962-8342
Fax: 202-962-8300

They publish a monthly newsletter with articles on industry statistics, regulations and NIMA events written by members and industry experts. Request from them a current list of infomercial production companies. This costs $150.

Following is a partial list of channels that run or will run infomercials:

Cable Channel/Network	**Headquarters**
ATV:Advertising TV	Cedar Grove, NJ
America's Talking	New York, NY
Booknet	New York, NY
Cable Health Club	Virginia Beach, VA
Cable Jazz Channel	Washington, D.C.
The Catalog Channel	(to be announced)
ESPN 2	Bristol, CT
The Eco Channel	Ellicot City, MD
FX	Los Angeles, CA
The Game Channel	Los Angeles, CA
The Game Show Channel	Virginia Beach, VA
Gaming & Entertainment Network	Culver City, CA
Golden American Network	Pittsburgh, PA
The Golf Channel	Beverly Hills, CA

Cable Channel/Network	Headquarters
H-TV, History TV Network	Birmingham, AL
Health & Fitness Network	New York, NY
The Health Channel	Providence, RI
The History Network	Washington, D.C.
Home & Garden TV Network	Cincinnati, OH
Magnet, Magazine Network	Los Angeles, CA
Military Channel	Louisville, KY
Network One	Los Angeles, CA
Newsport Television	Woodbury, NY
Ovation: Fine Arts Network	Alexandria, VA
Planet Central TV	Beverly Hills, CA
Q2	New York, NY
Recovery Network	Milwaukee, WI
TCI/BMG Music Channel	New York, NY
The Talk Channel	New York, NY
Talk TV Network	Phoenix, AZ
Television Food Network	New York, NY
The Therapy Channel	Los Angeles, CA
The TV Car Showroom	New York, NY
TV Macy's	New York, NY
Video Mall	(to be announced)
World African Network	Los Angeles, CA

Source these companies. Find out first, are they interested? How much will the production of the infomercial cost? Do they have blocks of time they have bought from channels? Can they refer you to a broker? You will also want to investigate the quality of their product and the way they do business. Most often you will hire them to produce the film, and they will help you get it on a channel.

In some cases, they buy you out and pay you a royalty. You lose control, but you will have made no cash investment. If you do not have any money, this may be your only option. However, you will also have to have a real gem of a product to lure a production company in this way. As always, the situation is the boss. The key is to proceed forward, no matter what. A list of infomercial companies that operate on a royalty basis follows:

American Telecast Corporation
16 Industrial Boulevard
Paoli Corporate Center
Paoli, PA 19301
215-251-0033

National Media Corp.
550 Pinetown Road
Ft. Washington, PA 19034
215-772-5160

Power Media Marketing Group
Jane Williams, President
150 East Olive Avenue
Suite 305
Burbank, CA 91502
818-557-8313
Fax: 818-557-8318

The Regal Group
1260 Virginia Drive
Ft. Washington, PA 19034
215-643-6300

USA Direct
12701 Whitewater Drive
Minnetonka, MN 55343
612-945-4000

NIMA also publishes helpful books including *NIMA—First Class Marketing 1993 National Infomercial Customer Survey*, a 60-page survey of 3,500 infomercial customers, and *InfoQuick Guide to Infomercials*, by Richard D. Bruno.

Pricing Infomercials Per 30 Minutes

Listed here you will find the current inventory stations offering of 30-minute infomercials and their *approximate* price per slot. The prices reflect early morning weekday, late night and some scattered weekend airings. Overnights are available at a discount. These prices are, of course, subject to change any time and are for comparison's sake only. Contact the stations for exact quotes on the times you may want. This is a guide only.

Location	Station	Affiliation	Price
Albany, NY	WRGB	CBS	$ 675
Albany, GA	WVGA	ABC	575
Albuquerque, NM	KZIA	IND	575
Allentown, PA	WFMZ	IND	850
Atlanta, GA	WTLK	IND	795
Atlanta, GA	WGNX	IND	1,750
Atlanta, GA	WVEU	IND	1,675
Augusta, GA	WRDW	CBS	575
Bakersfield, CA	KGET	NBC	975
Baltimore, MD	WNUV	IND	875
Baton Rouge, LA	WBTR	IND	626
Baton Rouge, LA	WGMB	FOX	1,050
Binghamton, NY	WICZ	NBC	1,350
Birmingham, AL	WABM	IND	750
Boston, MA	WHLL	IND	875
Boston, MA	WNDS	IND	1,175
Buffalo, NY	WKBW	ABC	795
Cedar Rapids, IA	KDUB	ABC	650
Chattanooga, TN	WDSI	FOX	795
Chicago, IL	WJYS	IND	895
Cleveland, OH	WOAC	IND	825
Columbus, GA	WXTX	FOX	575

Location	Station	Affiliation	Price
Corpus Cristi, TX	WXTX	NBC	$ 475
Davenport, IA	KLJB	FOX	525
Dayton, OH	WRGT	FOX	1,275
Detroit, MI	WADL	IND	2,550
El Paso, TX	KCIK	FOX	850
Erie, PA	WETG	IND	650
Fort Meyers, FL	WBR	IND	325
Fort Meyers, FL	WBBH	NBC	1,285
Fresno, CA	KAIL	IND	695
Grand Rapids, MI	WXMI	IND	775
Hartford, CT	WTWS	IND	1,550
Hartford, CT	WTXX	IND	1,975
Honolulu, HI	KBFD	IND	925
Huntsville, AL	WOWL	NBC	775
Huntsville, AL	WTRT	IND	495
Indianapolis, IN	WMCC	IND	895
Jackson, MI	WAPT	ABC	895
Jacksonville, FL	WAWS	IND	675
Jacksonville, FL	WBSG	IND	675
Joplin, MO	KOAM	CBS	795
Knoxville, TN	WKCH	FOX	1,175
Lansing, MI	WBSX	HSN	575
Las Vegas, NV	KFBT	IND	825
Las Vegas, NV	KRLR	IND	975
Los Angeles, CA	KAGL	IND	650
Los Angeles, CA	KVVT	IND	825
Louisville, KY	WDRB	FOX	695
Madison, WI	WKOW	ABC	1,450
Miami, FL	WBFS	IND	1,200
Miami, FL	WDZL	IND	1,375
Midland, TX	KTPX	NBC	850
Milwaukee, WI	WGCV	FOX	1,175
Mobile, AL	WPMI	FOX	695

Location	Station	Affiliation	Price
Monterey, CA	KCBA	FOX	$1,050
Montgomery, AL	WOOV	IND	895
Myrtle Beach, FL	WGSE	IND	550
Naples, Fl	WNPL	IND	625
Nashville, TN	WXMT	IND	1,525
New Orleans, LA	WVUE	ABC	1,975
New Orleans, LA	WNDS	FOX	1,575
New York, NY	WLIG	IND	1,750
New York, NY (Suburban)	WTZA	IND	1,275
Orlando, FL	WAYK	IND	695
Pensacola, FL	WEAR	ABC	950
Phoenix, AZ	KMOH	IND	675
Pittsburgh, PA	WNEU	IND	550
Raleigh-Durham, NC	WAAP	IND	450
Raleigh-Durham, NC	WYED	IND	550
Raleigh-Durham, NC	WRMY	IND	475
Reno, NV	KAME	FOX	1,150
Rockford, IL	WTVO	NBC	1,275
Sacramento, CA	KSCH	IND	1,375
Salt Lake City, UT	KOOG	IND	725
Salt Lake City, UT	KXIV	IND	815
San Francisco, CA	KCNS	IND	1,450
Sarasota, FL	WBSV	IND	675
Seattle, WA	KTTZ	IND	1,250
South Bend, IN	WHME	IND	850
St. Paul, MN	KLGT	IND	1,725
Syracuse, NY	WSYT	FOX	695
Tallahassee, FL	WTWC	NBC	975
Tampa, FL	WTMV	IND	675
Tampa, FL	WTTA	IND	795
Toledo, OH	WNWO	ABC	795

Location	Station	Affiliation	Price
Topeka, KS	KSNT	NBC	$ 625
Tulsa, OK	KOKI	FOX	1,795
West Palm Beach, FL	WTVX	IND	875
West Palm Beach, FL	WAQ	IND	775

Keeping Track of Recent Infomercial Trends

"And Now: Radio Infomercials! RAB and NIMA Huddle on Rules." *Mediaweek*, May 24, 1993. An article on the teaming up of NIMA and RAB to develop marketing guidelines for infomercials.

"Attention TV Shoppers: European Boom on the Horizon." *MultiChannel News*, September 20, 1993. An article on how the European direct response television market is poised for tremendous growth.

Bernard, Jami. "Extrasensory Programming." *New York Daily News*, August 1993. A commentary on the generous supply of infomercials for psychics.

Bone, Eugenia. "Invasion of the Infomercials." *Total TV*, August 14, 1993. An industry round-up article focusing on the popularity of infomercials.

Botton, Sari. "Sugarman's Infomercials: A Success Story." *HFFD*, July 19, 1993. A look at the success of Joe Sugarman and his "Blueblocker" sunglasses.

Chagollan, Steve. "The 19-Inch Mall." *Hollywood Reporter Special Report on Commercial Production*, June 1, 1993. An industry feature focusing mainly on how traditional ads agencies view the rise of the infomercial format.

Cooper, Jim. "Infomercials Welcomed Back into Ad Fold." *Broading & Cable*, May 24, 1992. Coverage of NIMA's mid-year meeting.

Cosby, Randall. "Surf's Up! Infomercials Making Waves in Advertising Industry." *Link: The Magazine of the Yellow Pages Medium*, June 1993. An in-depth story on the rising popularity of the infomercial.

Donaton, Scott. "Time Warner Studying Infomercials on Cable." *Ad Age*, June 7, 1993. A report on Time Warner's possible plans to use infomercials on its cable TV systems.

Elliot, Stuart. "Television Infomercial Products Are Beginning to Show Up on Some Well-Known Store Shelves." *The New York Times*, June 3, 1993. A column on infomercial products success in retail stores.

Finre, Niri. "Insanity TV." *Working Woman*, October 1993. An in-depth report on the industry, pegged to four of the most successful female celebrities.

Friedman, Arthur. "TV Infomercials Move Ahead in Ratings." *Women's Wear Daily*, June 9, 1993. A story on the growth of electronic retailing and how infomercials are changing.

Friedman, Wayne. "Infomercial Equity Offer." *Inside Media*, May 26, 1993. A report on the evolving relationship between infomercial companies and television stations.

Gallagher, Patricia. "Walking the Ever-Changing Line Between News and Advertising." *The Business Journalist*, Society of Business Editors and Writers, June 1993. Citing a program called "emerging public companies" that never made it on to CNBC because it bordered on touting stocks, the article suggests infomercials sometimes blur editorial and advertising content. The article also reports on the history of the industry, including past FTC actions against infomercials and NIMA-inspired reforms.

Geracimos, Ann. "Pizazz in the Pitch." *Washington Times*, August 9, 1993. An industry piece focusing on how infomercials have evolved from "old style" infomercials, which were all pitch into "slick sales scenarios".

Green, Lee. "Meet the Queen of Infomercials." *Spirit*, October 1993. A profile of Katie Williams, founder and CEO of Williams Television Time.

Hallen, Marx. "Why Not Take the Luck Out of Infomercials?" *DM News*, August 16, 1993. Hallen, former creative director at JWT Direct and Grey Direct, offers six ways to support an infomercial campaign.

Hawthorne, Tim. "As Seen on TV: The New World of Infomercials." A commentary on the past, present and future of infomercials.

"Infomercial Industry's Reputation Rising." *FTC Watch*, September 20, 1993. News item that mentions that acting Consumer Production Bureau Chief Chris White of FTC spoke at a NIMA meeting in London and had kind words for the industry's attempts to improve its reputation. Portions of White's speech are printed.

Hufstedar, P.J. "TV Trade." *Grand Junction Daily Sentinel*, July 18, 1993. An industry round-up piece focusing on the popularity of infomercials.

Kanner, Bernice. "Calling All Consumers." *New York Magazine*, October 4, 1993. A profile of Jeff Glickman, president of First Class Marketing.

Kenneally, Christopher. "Infomercial, News Show Receiving Mixed Reviews." *Electronic Media*, July 19, 1993. A story on

"New England Today," a paid-programming news magazine highlighting local Boston companies, produced by Boston-based Infovision.

Levin, Gary. "Big Marketers Will Reshape Infomercials." *Ad Age*, May 24, 1993. How major marketers are moving towards producing infomercials.

Levin, Gary. "The Infomercial as Steppingstone: Prepping for the Interactive Age." *Ad Age Special Report on Direct Response*, July 12, 1993. How advertising agencies and their direct response units view infomercials.

Levin, Gary. "Infomercials Are a Different Spin." *Ad Age*, September 20, 1993. An article on Slim-Fast Foods and Philips Consumer Electronics launching new infomercials.

Levine, Josh. "Entertainment or Deception." *Forbes*, August 2, 1993. An industry round-up piece focusing on the Fortune 500s and Madison Avenue agencies' growing acceptance of the infomercial format.

Matalon, Daniel. "Infomercials Invade the Mainstream." *The Financial Post*, "Canada's Business Voice," June 3, 1993. A report on the infomercial industry, both in the United States and in Canada.

Matsumoto, Nacy. "Amazing Discoveries by Infomercial Audiences." *Los Angeles Times*, August 26, 1993. A lengthy story detailing the behind the scenes look at the typical infomercial studio audience.

McCarroll, Thomas. "Attention TV Shoppers." *Time*, July 26, 1993. A story on the rise of home shopping, pegged to the QVC-HSN merger.

Morrow, Vicki. "Slice and Dice Ads for Mainstream." *Reuters*, Appeared in *Des Moines Register*, June 1, 1993. A report on the growth of the industry.

"Philips Infomercial Treads on Prime Time." *The Wall Street Journal*, September 22, 1993. An article reporting on how Philips Consumer Electronics infomercial "The Great Wall" is breaking new ground in the infomercial industry.

Purpura, Linda. "Pumping Up Sales with TV." *HFFD*, July 19, 1993. A round-up of the major fitness products offered through infomercials.

Purpura, Linda. "TV Stars—Infomercials Touted as Missing Link in Product Marketing Cycle." *HFFD*, June 14, 1993. A report on the increasing marketing value of the infomercial.

Pazzani, Martin. "Most Potent Marketing Tool Ever? The Underappreciated Infomercial." *Ad Age*, August 23, 1993. The senior VP at DDB Needham Worldwide comments on why the infomercial is appealing to marketers.

Quindlen, Anna. "1-800-Uh-Oh." *The New York Times*, June 9, 1993. A humorous commentary on the possible societal effects of TV Macy's by the well-known columnist.

Skalsky, C. and K. Stalter, "Direct Response TV." *Film and Video Production*, July 1993. A report on how commercial industry producers are crossing over to the infomercial industry.

Spiegel, Peter, and Marsha Rent. "Microcrisp: The Story Behind a Hit Infomercial." A behind-the-scenes look at the making of the Microcrisp infomercial.

Waters, Crystal. "Victoria Jackson: Not Just Another Pretty Face." *Home Office Computing*, June 1993. An article detailing Victoria Jackson's rise from garage-based business owner to infomercial star.

Wessel, Harry. "Half-Hour Infomercials Are Designed To Channel Viewer's Impulses into Sales." *Baltimore Sun*, June 13, 1993. An industry round-up piece focusing on why consumers purchase from infomercials, how consumers can protect themselves, recent FTC action against infomercials and an Orlando company cashing in on infomercials.

Yates, Jim. "As Consumers Change, So Does Advertising." *Direct Marketing*, July 1993. Touches on the most interesting points of Crain Communications' senior vice president Joe Cappo's address to NIMA's mid-year meeting in May, entitled "The slow and painful demise of advertising as we know it."

CHAPTER
8

Selling Online and Other Benefits of the Internet

Getting Online

The Internet is fast becoming an exceptional marketing opportunity. Aspects of communication from TV, telephones, newspaper and other media converge on this information highway. Even the Home Shopping Channel is online.

Sadly for far too many entrepreneurs, the Internet seems like some inscrutable nebula, which if approached will suck them into a perpetual confoundedness. I am here to tell you from personal experience that the information superhighway is super, but it is not in the least difficult to travel.

It had been seven years since I had any exposure to a computer. I jumped back into the cybernest just a few months ago. Visiting my local discount retail store, I bought a computer system, a Pentium 486 DX2, 100 MHz and 8MB of RAM, in December 1994. Do not let the gobbledygook of these numbers throw you. What they mean is that the computer is fast and has a lot of storage capability. The cost for the setup was approximately $4,000.

The ease of use and variety of programs absolutely dumbfounded me. I was up and running my new electronics in less than two hours. I even *understood* the instructions.

To start with, you need an online service, your gateway to the Internet ethers. I hooked up with Prodigy. For $2.50 a day I get more accessibility than I ever dreamed of.

Using the Internet To Research Your Field and Marketing Opportunities

Hey—it is not called the "information superhighway" for nothing. The Internet is chock-full of information, and information means opportunity. Information helps you sell because it gives you the edge. The more you know, the better you will be at beating everyone else to the punch.

One of the infinite conveniences of online services is the research capability. In conjunction with Prodigy, I connected to TimesLink (of the *Los Angeles Times*), a news and transaction information service with a database of thousands of back issues. This led me to the *Los Angeles Times* archives and changed the way I do research forever . . . just by the click of a mouse.

For example, I pulled up a search about home shopping channels or home shopping networks. Since 1993 there were more than 8,400 articles on the topics! Other sources for research via the Internet are many. Prodigy also offers a search feature called "Power Search" that includes the Associated Press database. The easiest way to get information and specific costs is to call Prodigy at 1-800-PRODIGY, and ask for a TimesLink or Prodigy start-up kit.

Understanding Home Pages and the World Wide Web

The World Wide Web is the section on the Internet where all the commerce takes place. Although it was designed as a state-of-the-art electronic marketplace, it can still accommodate some of the older electronic technologies like E-mail, FTP (file transfer protocol) and Gopher. Imagine a kind of enormous cybernetic swap-meet telescoping around the world. That's the Web.

To advertise and sell on the Web, you need to create a home page through home page developer. A *home page* is your presentation on the Internet. Consumers can locate it on the Web using a web browser. Located at a web site, home pages can contain text, graphics, still photos and even video. Obviously, the more complicated the home page, the higher the cost. We received quotes from three different home page developers ranging from $1,000 to $6,000. The old "you get what you pay for" does not necessarily hold true. We opted for the least expensive quote from Spinnet, and we are very satisfied. In addition to the initial $1,000, we have monthly provider costs of $300 (paid to CERFnet, which I will discuss more later). This includes a $50 maintenance fee to change copy and provides for one hour per month of work from Spinnet. If you are on-line, you may want to see what we get for that money. Our address is http://www.c3d.com.

Spinnet's offering is shown in Figure 8.1.

FIGURE 8.1
Spinnet Sales Brochure

Spinnet can help your business or organization take advantage of the Internet revolution. We can help with all aspects of World Wide Web development and implementation. From site design to integration with E-mail, Gopher and FTP, Spinnet can handle it all.

Web Site Design

Spinnet specializes in professional, innovative web site design. We design with both you and your user in mind, custom tailoring your web site to meet both of your needs. Spinnet will make sure that your pages look great no matter what types of browsers your customers are using.

Web Installation and Management

Spinnet can provide you with a complete World Wide Web solution, from initial design and web site creation to maintenance and expansion when you need to grow. We have an excellent relationship with CERFnet, the nation's premier Internet services provider, and can therefore offer you premium network and hardware services at reasonable prices.

Or, if you prefer, Spinnet can install your web site on the server of your choice, either at a Web service provider like CERFnet, or on your own in-house server. We can handle all aspects of server setup, including purchase and installation of computer hardware and software. Or, we may be

Source: Reprinted by permission of Spinnet, Inc.

FIGURE 8.1, *continued*
Spinnet Sales Brochure

able to work with hardware your company may currently use for other purposes.

Graphics

Spinnet can handle all of your graphics needs. Our in-house staff can adapt your company's existing artwork, or create new graphics based on your chosen theme and style. If you prefer, we can work with the graphic artist of your choice to create artwork that looks great on the Web. Spinnet understands the special needs of Web-based artwork, ensuring that your graphics look great and download as rapidly as possible.

Other Services

Often it makes sense to integrate your website with other Internet protocols like Gopher, FTP TELNET or E-mail autoresponders. Spinnet has the expertise to set up and manage multi-protocol sites that take advantage of the unique strengths of these different protocols, integrating them into a complete package.

Flexible Working Relationship

If you want to handle some aspects of your web site yourself while passing other responsibilities onto us, Spinnet can provide a custom solution to fit your particular situation.

FIGURE 8.1, *continued*
Spinnet Sales Brochure

Pricing

Since every website we design is a custom job, we have provided an on-line form (see our World Wide Web site at http://www.spinnet.com/) for you to tell us about your project. We'll take this information and give you a cost estimate for your specific project. You can even tell us roughly what you're willing to spend and we'll suggest ways to make your web site fit your budget.

Talk to us. Every situation is unique. Ask questions, tell us about your plan and let us help design a custom solution to fit your needs.

We've tried to make it as easy as possible for you to contact us. If you can't find your favorite mode of communication below, we'd be interested to hear about it.

World Wide Web

Visit our World Wide Web site at http://www.spinnet.com/. If you're looking for a price estimate for the web site you have in mind, use our on-line questionnaire to tell us about your plans. We'll get back to you with a cost estimate.

Electronic Mail

You can reach Spinnet via E-mail at info@spinnet.com, or use our E-mail right from your web browser. We're fully mime capable, so feel free to send graphics and other enclosures.

FIGURE 8.1, *continued*
Spinnet Sales Brochure

Postal Service

If you're a mail traditionalist, you can contact Spinnet by surface mail at:

Spinnet, Inc.
10946 Welsh Road
San Diego, CA 92126

Telephone

Give us a phone call at 619-507-0795.

Facsimile

Our fax number is 619-530-0276.

Sample Home Page

Your opening page should be an attention-grabber. It should reveal a minimal amount of information about your products along with some graphics and photos. The viewer may then pick and choose the subsequent pages based on his or her interest. Our home page on the Internet's World Wide Web, developed by Spinnet, is shown in Figure 8.2.

FIGURE 8.2
C3D Sports Home Page

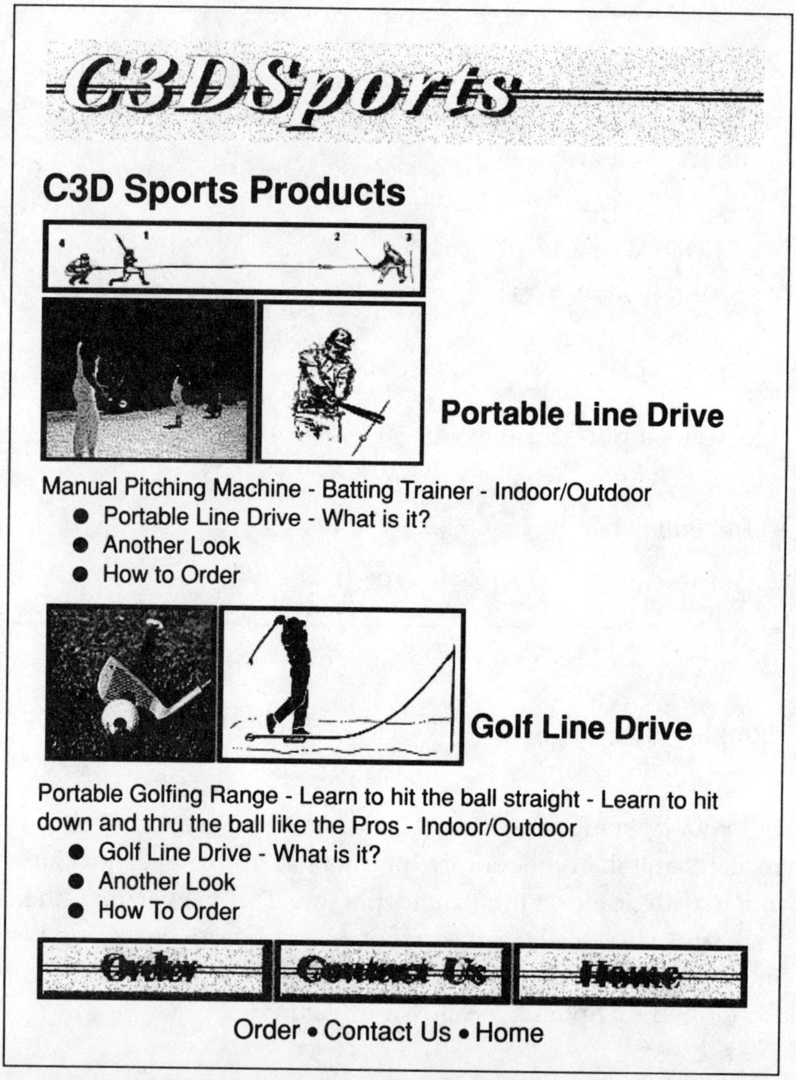
C3DSports
C3D Sports Products
Portable Line Drive
Manual Pitching Machine - Batting Trainer - Indoor/Outdoor
● Portable Line Drive - What is it?
● Another Look
● How to Order
Golf Line Drive
Portable Golfing Range - Learn to hit the ball straight - Learn to hit down and thru the ball like the Pros - Indoor/Outdoor
● Golf Line Drive - What is it?
● Another Look
● How To Order
Order
Contact Us
Home
Order • Contact Us • Home

FIGURE 8.2, *continued*
C3D Sports Home Page

C3DSports

C3D Sports - Portable Line Drive

Over 30,000 units sold to University and High School Coaches!

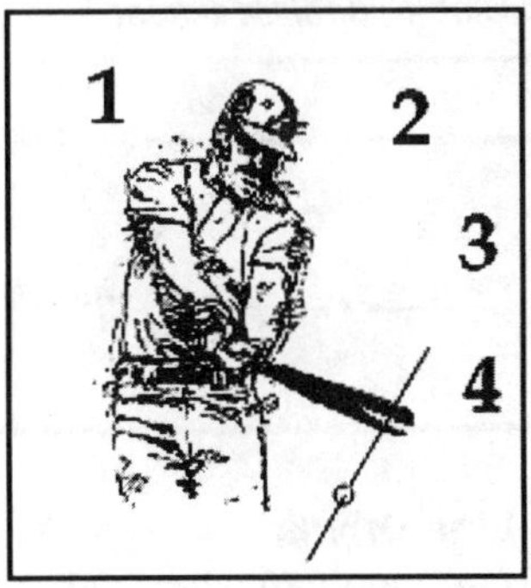

How It Works

- 1. Hitter takes a normal swing and does not start with the bat on the cable.
- 2. **Line Drive** forces the hitter to carry their hands in a high strong position throughout the swing.
- 3. It requires the hitter to have square hands at impact.
- 4. Forces the hitter to have a long bat through the ball. This creates important muscle memory for a proper swing.

Other Features

- New improved bat — more wood on the top of the groove than below; keeps the batter on top of the ball. 80% of all missed pitches are swung on below the ball!
- Every pitch delivered at a different speed to varying areas of the strike zone; pitch to pitch and a bat that forces the batter to be on top of the ball!
- **600** pitches per hour at **100** mph or **10** mph.
- Batting practice **on game day** — home or away!
- Indoor/Outdoor

FIGURE 8.2, *continued*
C3D Sports Home Page

C3DSports

C3D Sports - Portable Line Drive Another Look

Over 30,000 units sold to University and High School Coaches!

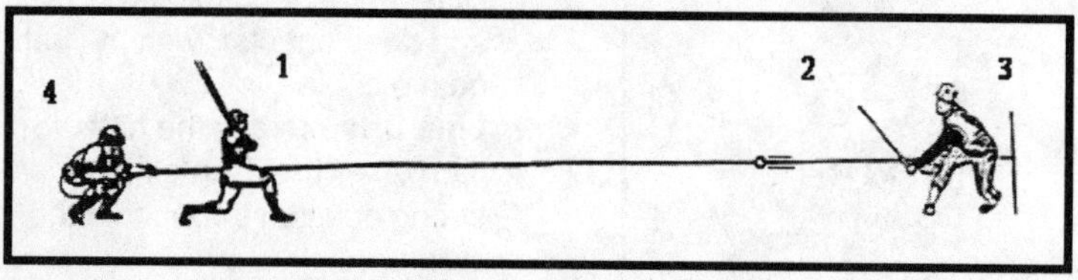

- **1.** Remember 7 out of 10 hits are **Line Drives.**
- **2.** Fiberglass pitch stick is used so anyone can pitch 100 mph to 10 mph easily.
- **3.** Cable hooks up to anything stable, indoors or out; pole, tree, fence, doorknob, etc.
- **4.** Catcher holds one end of the cable and may move the line for simulation of curves, sliders, or the rise ball.

Other Features

- Use behind the dugout during games pitching 5 to 6 mph faster than what they are seeing live in the game. Players now track the ball easily.
- Batting practice on game day or home or away with portable **Line Drive.**

FIGURE 8.2, *continued*
C3D Sports Home Page

C3DSports

C3D Sports - Portable Line Drive- What Is It?

It is a plastic coated steel cable, 35' long. One end of the cable attaches to anything stable. The other end of the cable is held by anyone in a catching position (no equipment is necessary). There is a plastic ball that slides along the cable and it is propelled down the line using a *fiberglass pitch stick.*

The *key* to the product is the *bat.* It is a full wood bat with a groove cut out of the middle, so it looks like a clothespin, if you look at it from the side. The important thing is that the groove is slightly off centered, with more wood on top of the groove than below. This teaches the batter to stay *on top of the ball.* As the ball is propelled down the line, the batter takes a normal swing at the ball. If it is a good swing, the cable will pass through that groove and the batter will hit the ball back up that line. *600 swings per hour.*

You may also play a game taking turns hitting.

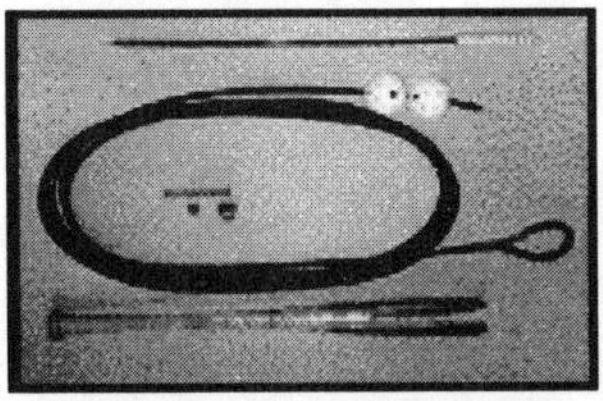

Contents per Unit or Set

- One grooved bat
- 35 ft of steel coated airline cable
- Fiberglass pitch stick
- Ball
- Hardware
- Instructions and batting tips

FIGURE 8.2, *continued*
C3D Sports Home Page

C3DSports

C3D Sports - Golf Line Drive

I will endorse Golf Line Drive with 100% conviction because I've already seen the results... Golfers improve their ability to hit the ball straight. We are using Golf Line Drive at our golf schools because it can help accomplished players, juniors and beginners. It works for everyone regardless of skill level.

—Coach Daugard

Features

- Learn to hit the ball straight
- No bending over to tee up the ball
- No retrieving balls
- No nets
- 3 days to a great swing
- Indoor/Outdoor — 365 day season

FIGURE 8.2, *continued*
C3D Sports Home Page

C3DSports

C3D Sports - Another Look

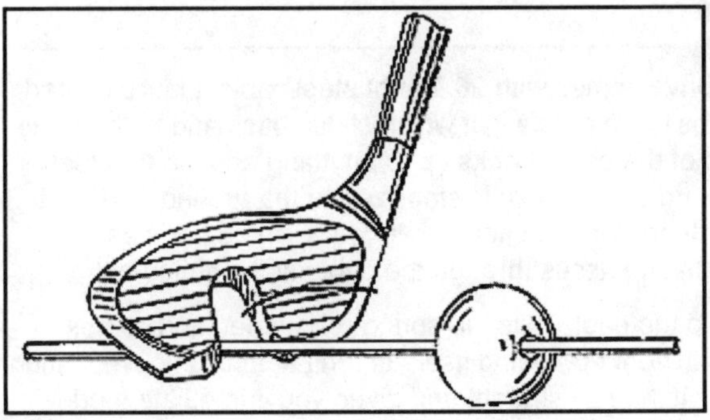

Features

- Specially grooved golf iron
- Instructional video included by Jim Colbert, shot by ESPN
- Learn to hit the ball **straight**
- It teaches you to lay the center of the club face on the back of the ball while teaching you how to hit down and through the ball — the Number One requirement in golf
- **Line Drive Forces the above**

FIGURE 8.2, *continued*
C3D Sports Home Page

C3DSports

C3D Sports - Golf Line Drive - What Is It?

The Golf Line Drive comes with 26 feet of steel cable, plastic coated, and has a golf ball with a hole in it which slides back and forth on the cable. One end of the cable hooks up to anything about 5 to 6 feet high; the other end of the cable is stabilized to the ground with a small stake outdoors, or a suction cup indoors. The 5 iron has a groove in it so that it passes through the cable striking the ball.

The ball goes up the cable, hits the spring rebounder, and comes back as fast as it went up, teeing itself up... hit again. Quick repetition teaches you to hit the ball straight and gives you immediate feed-back. If you don't hit the ball correctly, the cable will wobble. You may set up anywhere, indoor, or out, where you can safely swing your new iron.

You will get 150 swings in 15 minutes. Getting that kind of practice will take strokes off your game.

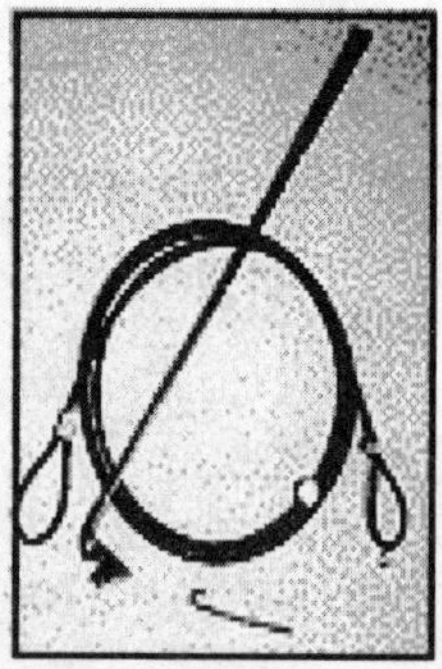

Contents per Unit or Set

- Specially grooved golf iron
- 26' 3000 lb. test airline coated steel cable
- Golf ball
- Spring loaded rebounder
- End hook for attaching
- Steel ground stake for outdoor use
- Suction cup for indoor use
- Lock loop
- Complete instructions and golf tips by Jim Colbert

FIGURE 8.2, *continued*
C3D Sports Home Page

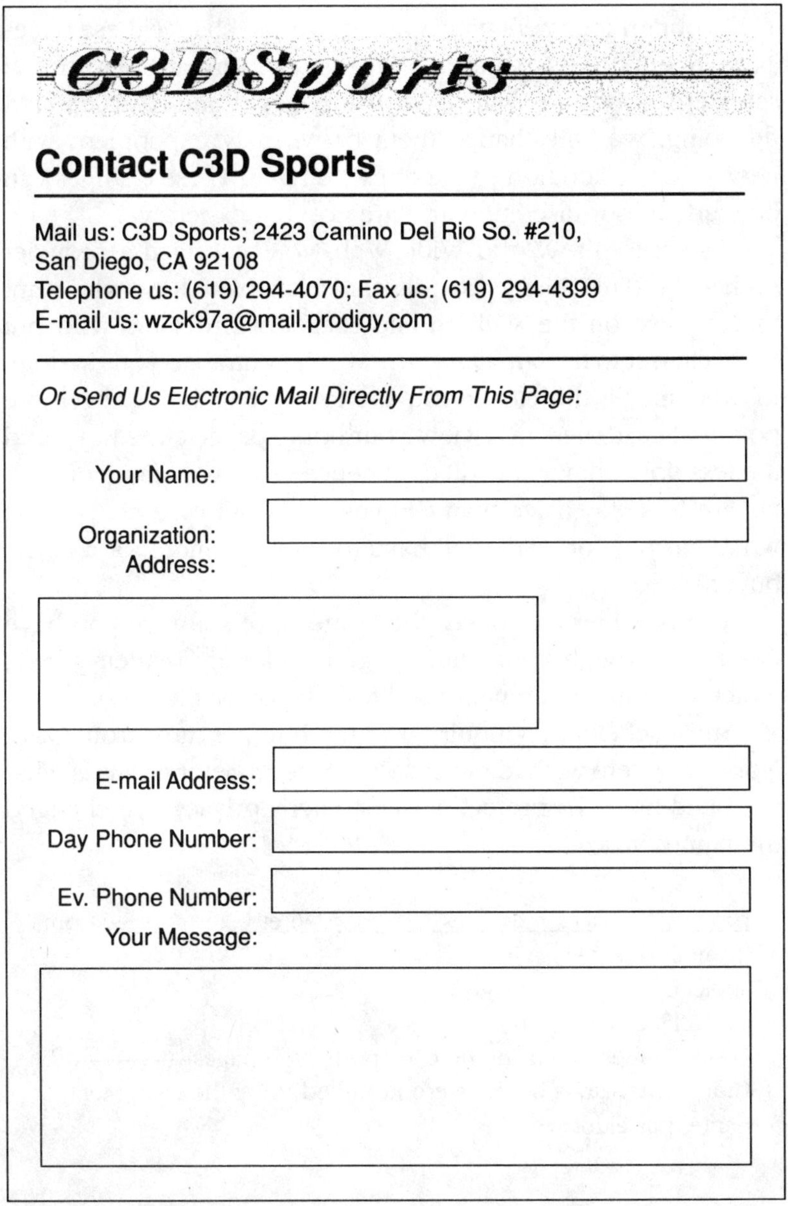

C3DSports

Contact C3D Sports

Mail us: C3D Sports; 2423 Camino Del Rio So. #210,
San Diego, CA 92108
Telephone us: (619) 294-4070; Fax us: (619) 294-4399
E-mail us: wzck97a@mail.prodigy.com

Or Send Us Electronic Mail Directly From This Page:

Your Name:

Organization:

Address:

E-mail Address:

Day Phone Number:

Ev. Phone Number:

Your Message:

Getting Results

In our arrangement with Spinnet, we can change these pages as we deem necessary based on feedback from sales statistics. If sales are good, we will leave the pages alone. If sales start dropping, we will change them or we may experiment with new pages in addition to the ones we have. These changes can be made at our discretion and are not that expensive.

To access the World Wide Web, you will need a provider such as CERFnet. Many providers are available. Those who want to advertise on the Web should seek out providers who put them closest to the *backbone*, the Web's central nervous system. In web-speak, the closer you get to the backbone, the more potential customers may view your home page at one time, and the less down time you will experience. Although many providers are less expensive than CERFnet, this is a case of "you get what you pay for." You will have to shell out more for a larger buyer base.

The provider introduces the home page software you have designed through your home page developer via their *server*, which is actual equipment used to link you to the Web.

Surprise! Our first inquiry over the Internet came from Oslo, Norway, where we had never sold products before. This is what it looked like. (To protect our customer's privacy, we changed the names and address.)

prodigy® services messages 5/26 et 3:04 pm
from: cerf 'n'web
subject: internet message
date: 05/23 06:36 am
————message from the c3d sports web pages————
(note: any blanks below were not filled in by the customer)
name: pat eldor

address: even 83 7241c oslo norway
e-mail address: pst.even@norway
phone: 123-1234
——————————message——————————
please send all info on your products asap
____

Another surprise! Our sixth response from Sweden was a customer wanting to distribute in Europe for us.

prodigy (services messages 6/04 et 11:14 am
from: cerf 'n'web
subject: Message from C3D Website
date: 6/04 7:15 am
————message from the c3d sports web pages————
(note: any blanks below were not filled in by the customer)
name: Sven Stennis
address: Oxhagsvaegan 20 143 80 Stockholm Sweden
email address: pst.Stennis@kojj.se
phone: 48 9 88 09
——————————message——————————
please send all info on your products asap
____

Comparison of Internet and Home Shopping Channel Sales

I can make some comparison of Internet and home shopping channel sales based on experience. As is always true in sales, *the situation is the boss*. It is not so much a matter of one sales method being better overall as it is of optimizing sales from a broader spectrum of possibilities. If you augment your home shopping advertising base with an Internet home page, it could definitely increase your sales, as long as your Internet arrangement does not conflict with your TV station guidelines.

Each has advantages and disadvantages. Internet marketing gives you more personal control and optimizes cash flow. On the other hand, since there are many more people watching TV at the present time than there are online through the Internet, home shopping offers the larger exposure. The Internet still does not have the shopper appeal of television; you have to rely on consumers who have both time and the Internet aptitude to comb the Web for deals. It is definitely more of a crap shoot, but it does provide reasonably priced international exposure. See Figures 8.3 and 8.4 for checklists outlining the elements to consider in each of these marketing opportunities.

Manufacturing

For either the Internet or home shopping, manufacturing is basically the same. However, the timing, flow and volume requirements are different. You can do your manufacturing for Internet customers after the end sale. This eliminates much risk. By contrast, for home shopping you must produce before the end sale. The station may return product that it cannot readily sell. The flow for the Internet will be more even since the sales are daily, versus broad sales made on home shopping channels only within a short time. Home shopping venues may be more uneven and less controlled. However, you will probably have lower storage costs if you use on-time delivery (basically manufacturing after the wholesaler orders).

Sales

Internet sales are retail; that is, the sell is to the end buyer. Home shopping sales are wholesale; the sell is to the retailer.

Some companies do not want to sell retail. In the past, there were huge costs for huge exposure. Neither the Internet or home shopping require a storefront. However, sellers may still prefer the volume they get from home shopping sales, which may parallel traditional wholesale sales, to Internet fits and starts. Volume sales reduce cost per unit. This, of course, depends on large and small product runs costs.

Collections

With home shopping, all collections are taken care of by the channel or network. You only have to get one check from them. However, with Internet sales you are responsible for making collections one at a time. All this takes many hours. Plus, any bad debt reverts back to you.

Shipping

The situation with shipping is similar to that for collections, comparison-wise. You ship directly to the home shopping network, and they are responsible for all shipping costs. This includes shipping to the buyer and returns. With the Internet, these responsibilities are yours.

Special Costs

With home shopping, special costs may be found in the areas of uneven labor hours, overtime, sales costs and travel. The Internet options are the initial set-up, which consists of programming and a provider.

Interactive Shopping Network

If, after reading this, you are still too befuddled to move into online marketing, try the Interactive Shopping Network (ISN).

FIGURE 8.3
Project Home Shopping

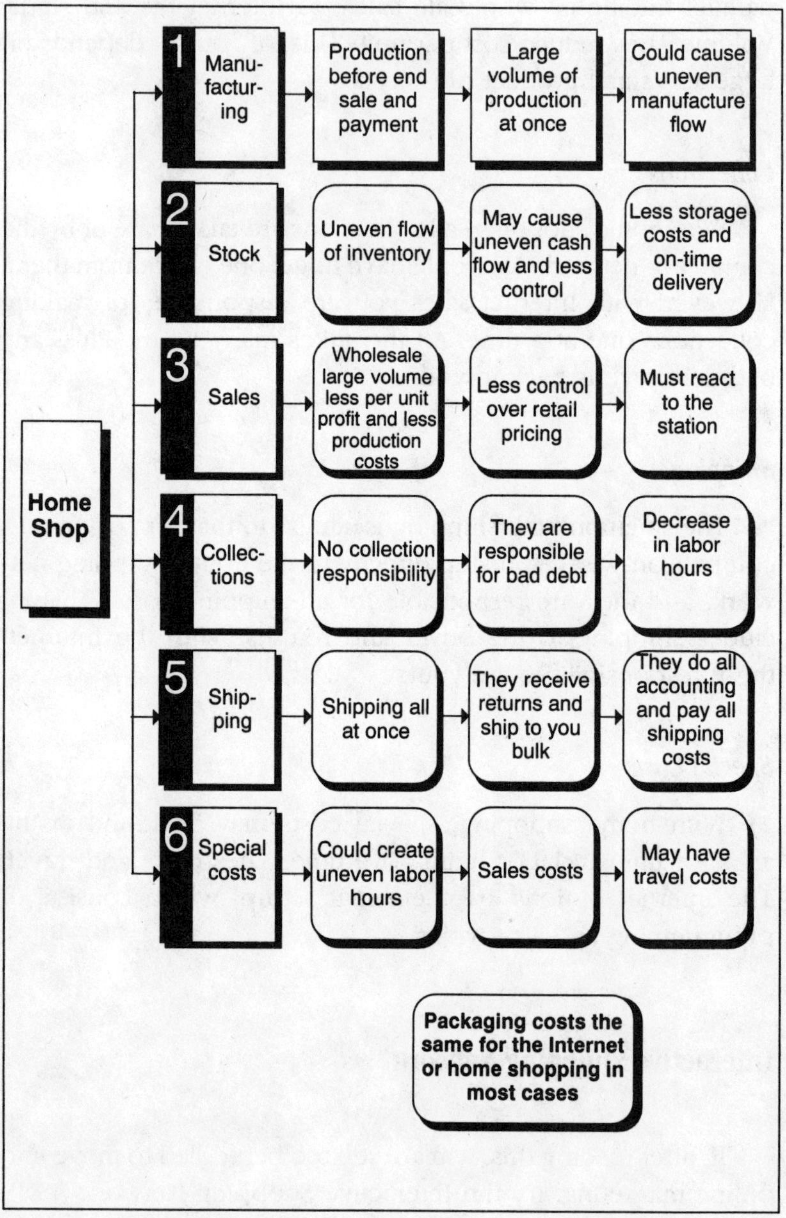

FIGURE 8.4
Project Internet

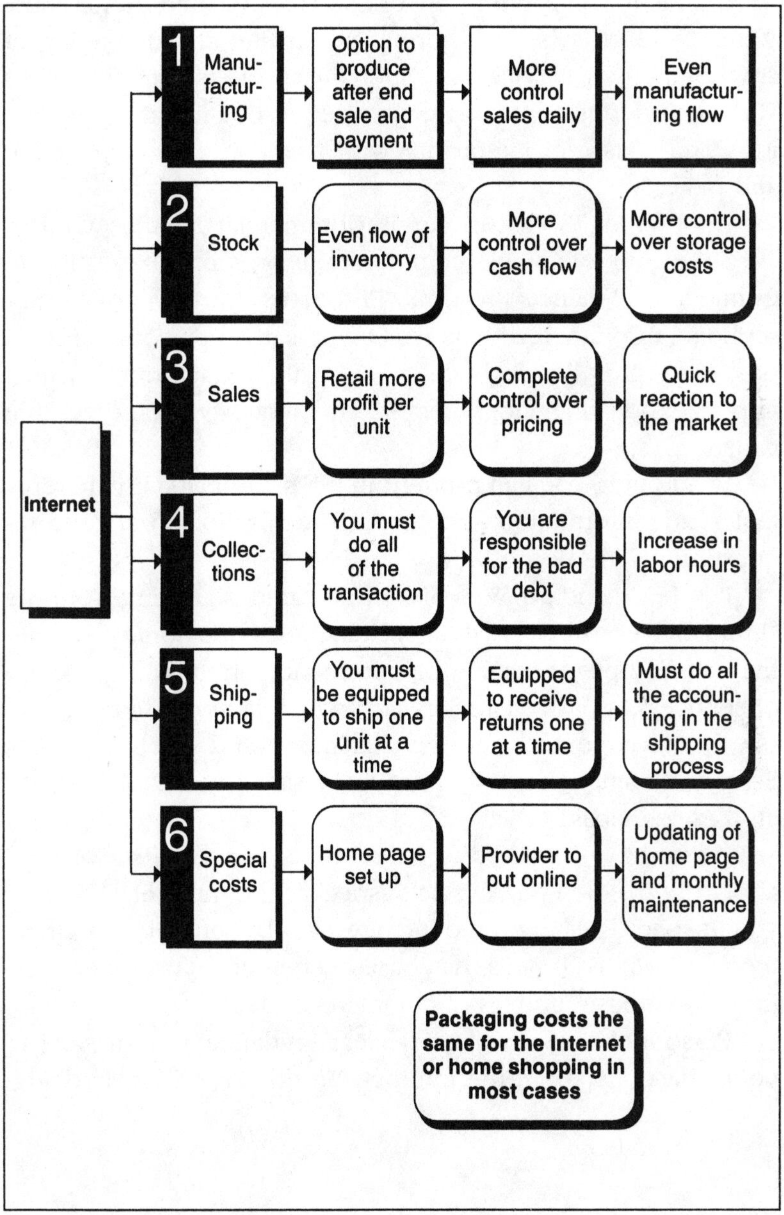

This outfit will put your product on the Internet for as low as $60 per year. It accepts Visa, MasterCard and American Express.

Interactive Shopping Network services include professional World Wide Web site authoring, publishing and marketing of any company it services. Additionally, it offers a menu full of Web option tools for taking orders, requesting literature, receiving comments and interacting with users who view your site and pages.

Another of ISN's services is Commercial Finance Online. Targeted to the business community, it promotes education in Commercial Finance Products, Resources and Solutions. Subscribers of Commercial Finance Online can participate in E-mail posted to the following categories: banking, factoring, leasing, import/export financing, mergers and acquisitions and venture capital.

In addition, you can profit from ISN's automatic E-mail reply that sends information about your organization to anyone requesting it. You do nothing.

ISN has standard Web Site opportunities ranging from the "Premier Web Site Service" (which includes one home page and five detailed pages containing information about your products or services), to "Web Lite Service" (which is more succinct with one home page and one detailed page) and "Web Ultra Lite Service" (a single home page). Business support tools support all these services.

If you have hesitated to get a home page because you fret about the needle in a haystack aspect of the Internet, ISN is for you. It specializes in promoting new sites by sending announcements to key web sites, databases, directories and other locations that house indexes of commercial sites.

Personnel at ISN will offer clear guidance and answers to your questions about the Internet, World Wide Web, and suggest how it may benefit you and your company. After assessing your needs, they then provide a cost-effective solution:

E-mail: help@cfonline.com
Tel: 206-343-1236
Fax: 206-343-1233

CHAPTER 9

Creating New Products for TV Using "Mind Maps"

Taking Advantage of Cycles in Home Shopping

Home shopping—both in regular and infomercial format—has gone through two cycles. The first cycle featured products typically sold by demonstration at fairs, rallies and swap meets. The second cycle featured products that had not succeeded in the retail arena because they required, and did not get, demonstration, or because they did not get enough exposure.

Home shopping is about to enter a third cycle, the most exciting to date. It will feature new products developed specifically for TV sales.

In response to this trend, I have developed a system I call "Mind Maps," a technique for conceiving new ideas for TV products. This technique issues from the "nothing new under the sun" idea. Most ideas are not really "new," but rather they are combinations and modifications of old ideas. The illustration shown in Figure 9.1 is there to encourage you to keep in mind the following ways to think creatively:

- If you follow a heavily traveled road, you will never pass the person in front of you.
- If you come to a *Y* in the road, always take the road less traveled.
- Construct new roads in lieu of traveling a beaten path.
- The measure of a person is that person's will to resist. Therefore, choices where the road is not heavily traveled will always be harder to follow but will reap larger rewards when you reach your destination. Resist that beaten path.

Think about it. We most often view products as a whole rather than as separate parts. However, if you are able to look at the details of any given product and extrapolate new features from there, a wide range of invention quickly reveals itself. Mind Maps asks you to look at the parts, the details. By breaking products into segments and asking questions about those segments, we can gain insight for improving existing products and conceiving innovative new ones.

Remember that anything is only as good as its least desirable aspect. Your challenge as a creator is to make even your worst creations good.

Project 1: Synonym Method

As an exercise, put the word *ball* in the middle of a circle. Using the thesaurus and dictionary, fill in the first ring of circles around the word "ball" with synonyms and related words. This kind of free association will loosen the boundaries of traditional whole-product observation.

FIGURE 9.1
Mind Map

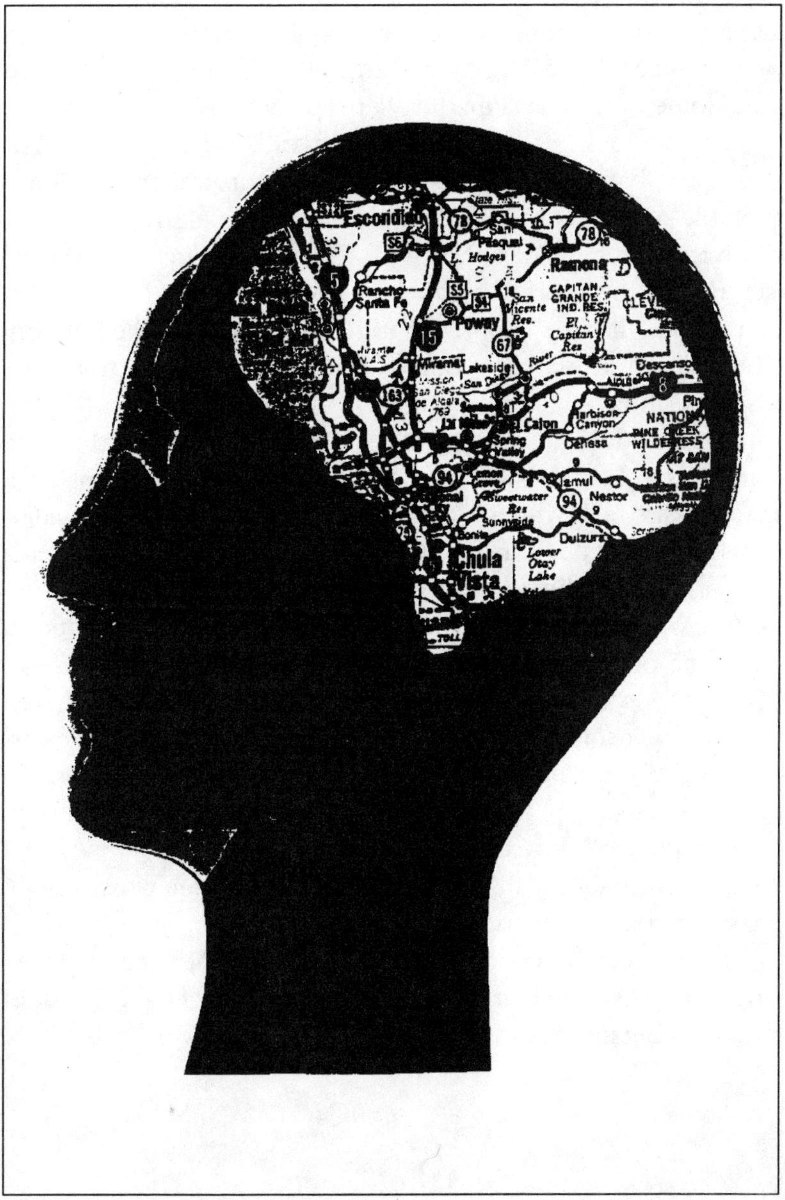

Then, again using the thesaurus and dictionary, fill in a second ring of circles with synonyms for the words in the first ring. Some of the definitions will lead you back to *ball*. Others will have numerous synonyms. Use as many circles in the outer ring as you want. Your objective is to find as many words as you can. Some of the ideas that may ensue are shown in Figure 9.2.

Finally, look at combinations of words for new ideas. For example, "ball-globe-map of Earth." Of course, there are innumerable globes on the market, also inflatable globe balls.

Next, combine "ensphere-ball." A new product on the market now is a colorful silky cloth covering over ballons—an "ensphere." It has a pull-string to tighten it around the balloon. The balloon lasts longer because of the cloth protection. It is also reusable.

Another idea that suggests itself is a ball combined with a curve—the "wiffle ball." The "jet ball" is an eyeball inside a clear plastic ball, which is filled a little over halfway with water. Because the eyeball inside is bottom heavy, the pupil and iris part of the eye always appear to be looking up, floating in the water. When you roll the ball, the eyeball stays suspended in the same position. It just keeps staring upwards.

Applying Mind Map and using the words "eye-ball-ensphere," we see the inspiration for added physical qualities such as transparency of the outer ball, bottom-heavy eyeball and water.

Now let's adapt the concept to a variation, "heavenly body-ball-ensphere." How about putting bobbing planets inside the transparent ball and filling it with colored water which might make the ball more appealing?

Free association and variation are the crux of Mind Maps. As you begin thinking this way, you will probably get a real rush of new combinations and ideas.

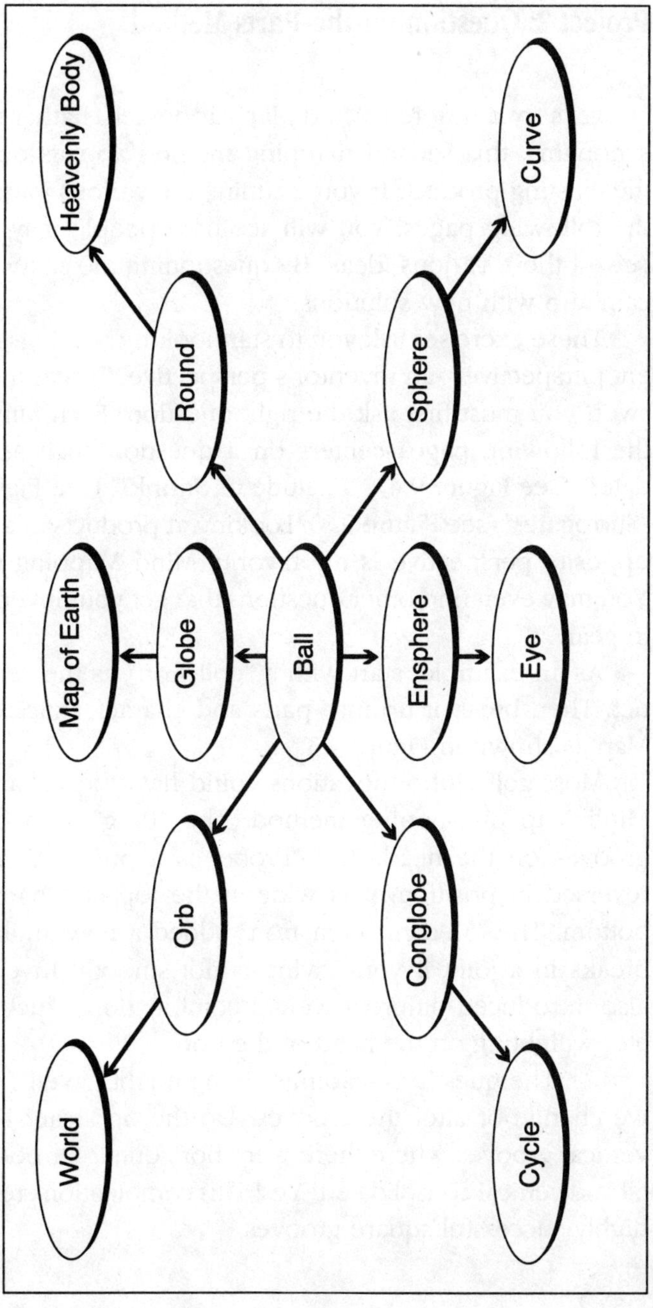

FIGURE 9.2
Mind Map: Synonym Method

Project 2: Questioning-the-Parts Method

Let's try a different Mind Maps approach. Rather than using synonyms, this second mapping method applies questions to the existing product. If you examine the various Mind Maps on the following pages, you will see how people may have conceived these various ideas. By questioning the status quo, they came up with new solutions.

These exercises ask you to start looking at things in a different perspective—an inventor's perspective. To get the right answer, you must first ask the right question. Each Mind Map on the following pages centers on a question such as "Consolidate?" (see Figure 9.4), "Exclude or Shrink?" (see Figure 9.6) or "Surrogate?" (see Figure 9.8). Looking at products in a reverse or opposite perspective is my favorite Mind Mapping technique. You may even find other questions that get your inventor's mind in gear.

As an example, start with a "golf iron" as the central product. Then break it up into parts and characteristics on a Mind Map as shown in Figure 9.3.

Most golf club innovations could have been based on the Mind Map questioning method. The "Ping" club has square grooves on the head. The "Probe" is a putter with the shaft reversed in position; it is wide at the top and narrow at the bottom. The "Medicus Golf Iron" added a new angle. Its shaft breaks in a joint if your swing is not smooth. Inventors have also introduced different weight combinations, such as perimeter weighting on the head of the iron.

The questions leading to Ping might have been: Should we change or alter the grooves? Do the opposite? How about vertical grooves where there were horizontal? Or both horizontal and vertical consolidated? Yes! This combination created Ping's highly successful square grooves.

FIGURE 9.3
Mind Map: Questioning-the-Parts Method

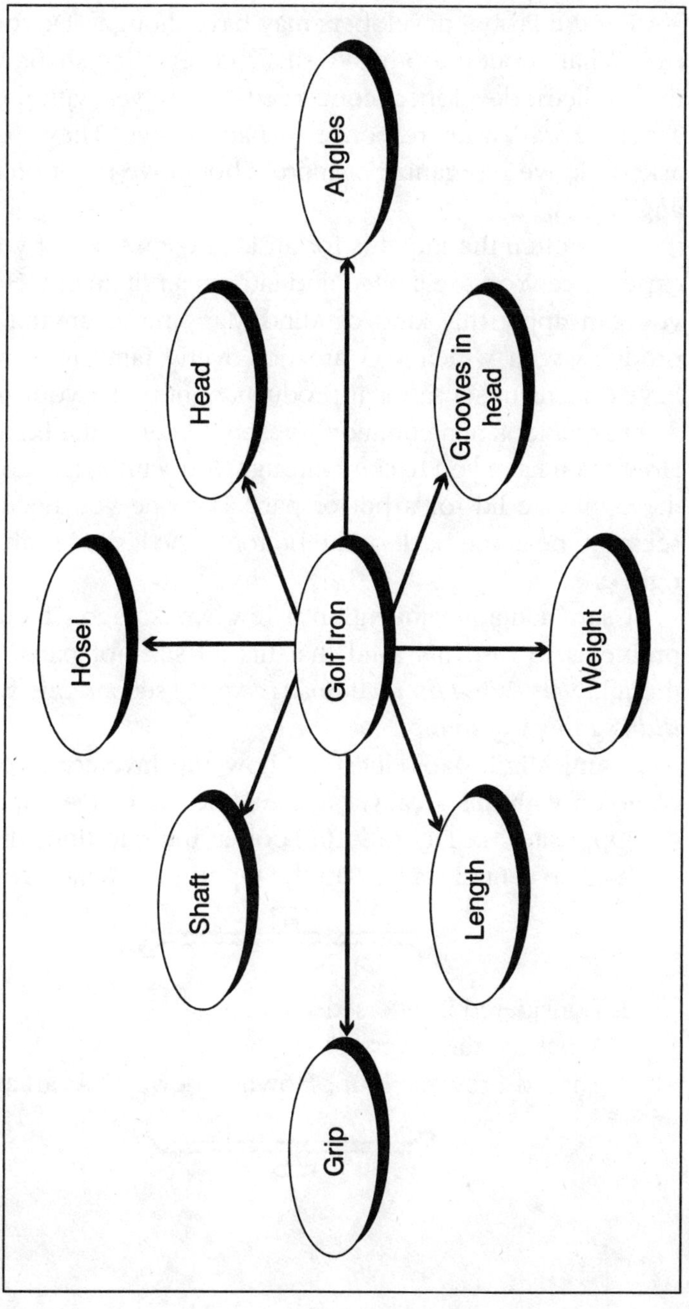

For the Probe, developers may have thought: Do the opposite? What about a top-heavy shaft? Reverse the shaft? Yes. For the Medicus, developers concerned themselves with producing a sort of Pavlovian response to bad swings. They may have asked, do we reorganize or more? Should we put it on another angle? Yes.

Most often the impetus for an idea comes out of your own experience. You see a need and fathom a fulfillment. However, you can apply this kind of Mind Mapping to anything, even products with which you are not overly familiar. You might have dozens of sensational products right under your nose.

Take a look at a common household item—the lid to a pan. How often have you hacked through your cupboard looking for the right size lid for a pot or pan? The one you need always seems to be at the back or the bottom. The last lid is always the right one.

I saw a unique invention a few weeks ago. It put all lid problems to rest. It's a lid that fits all sizes of pans. My first thought was, *What an ingenious idea*! My second one was, *Why didn't I think of that*?

Using Mind Maps, let's see how the inventor might have come up with this idea. Go to the Mind Map page entitled "Do the Opposite?" in Figure 9.10. Look at the questions that circle around the central issue, "Do the Opposite?" Which apply?

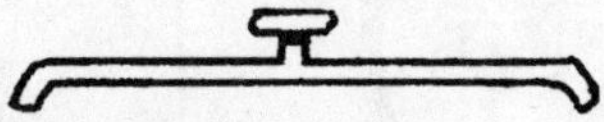

1. Considered it reversed?
2. What are the reverses?
3. Should I reverse it up? Down? Sideways? At an angle?

My thought process using the "Do the opposite?" Mind Map was as follows. First I considered it reversed up.

Then with a reversed handle. The only reverse I see is "up." So should I reverse it? Yes, up. Down? Down does not apply. Sideways? No, again. How about at an angle?

Maybe. I am on to something. Wait: My lid does not work. It is recessed too far down into the pan. It's easy to see that less angle will pull the center of the lid up.

Next, we go to the Mind Map (shown in Figure 9.12) "Reorganize or More?" What led me to where I am now? "Reverse" and "at an angle." Is there more reverse? No. More angle? Maybe more angles?

No, still fits one pan. More angles?

Yes, it now fits all sizes of pans and does not recess too far down into the pan.

So we can see how the Mind Map process works by applying it after the fact. Doing these exercises will force you to start looking at products from a fresh perspective.

The inventor of the Topsy Tail, the highly successful hair ornament, personifies the success of thinking from a different perspective. She has dyslexia. She claimed on TV that her impairment helped her come up with the invention; it is easy for her to make observations from different angles because of her handicap. She has made millions with this simple product. This led "Lifestyles of the Rich and Famous" to feature her on their program.

Creating New Ideas Using Mind Maps

Figures 9.4 through 9.21 on the following pages incorporate Mind Map questions to hone or refine product ideas along with blank Mind Maps to use for *your* winning ideas.

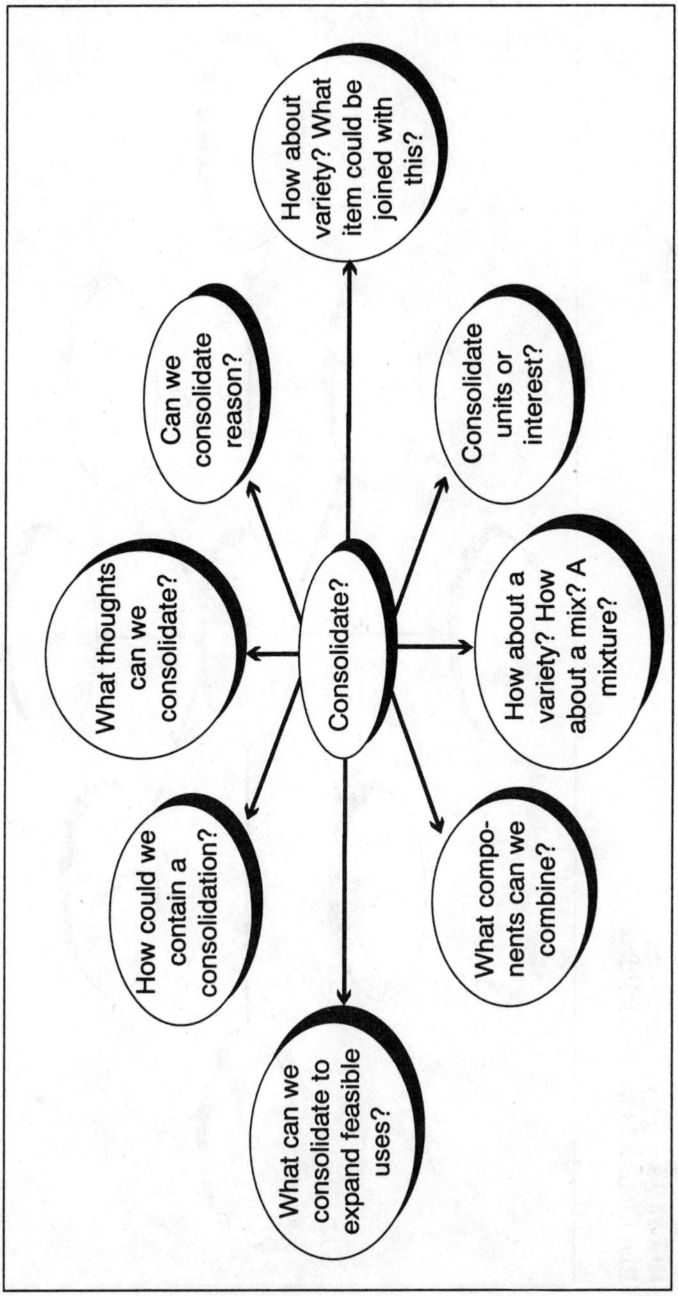

FIGURE 9.4
Mind Map: Consolidate

FIGURE 9.5
Blank Mind Map: Consolidate?

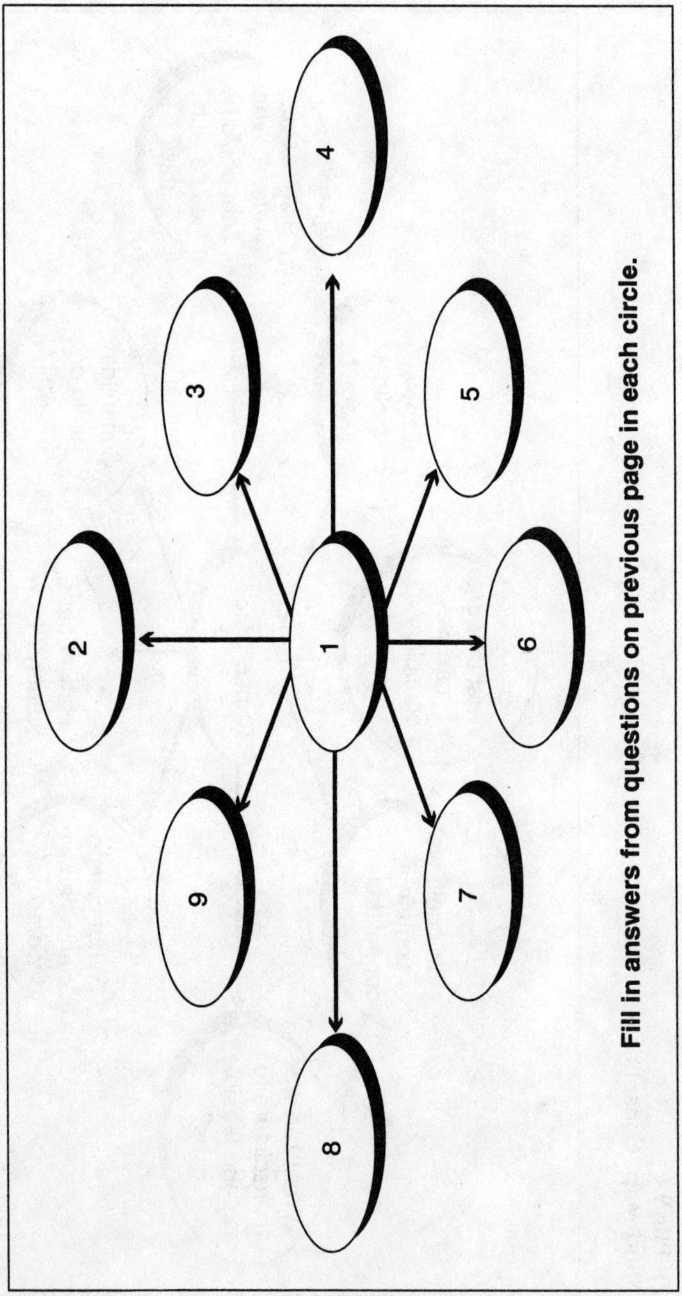

FIGURE 9.6
Mind Map: "Exclude or Shrink?"

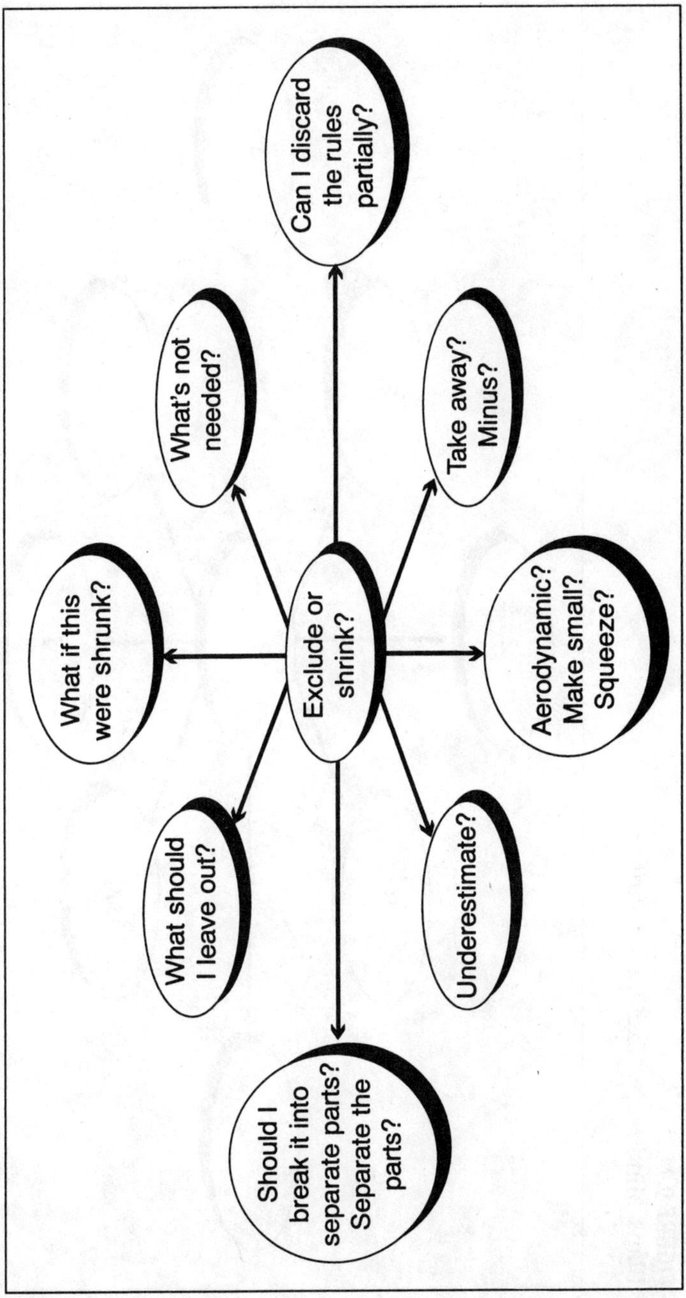

FIGURE 9.7
Blank Mind Map: "Exclude or Shrink?"

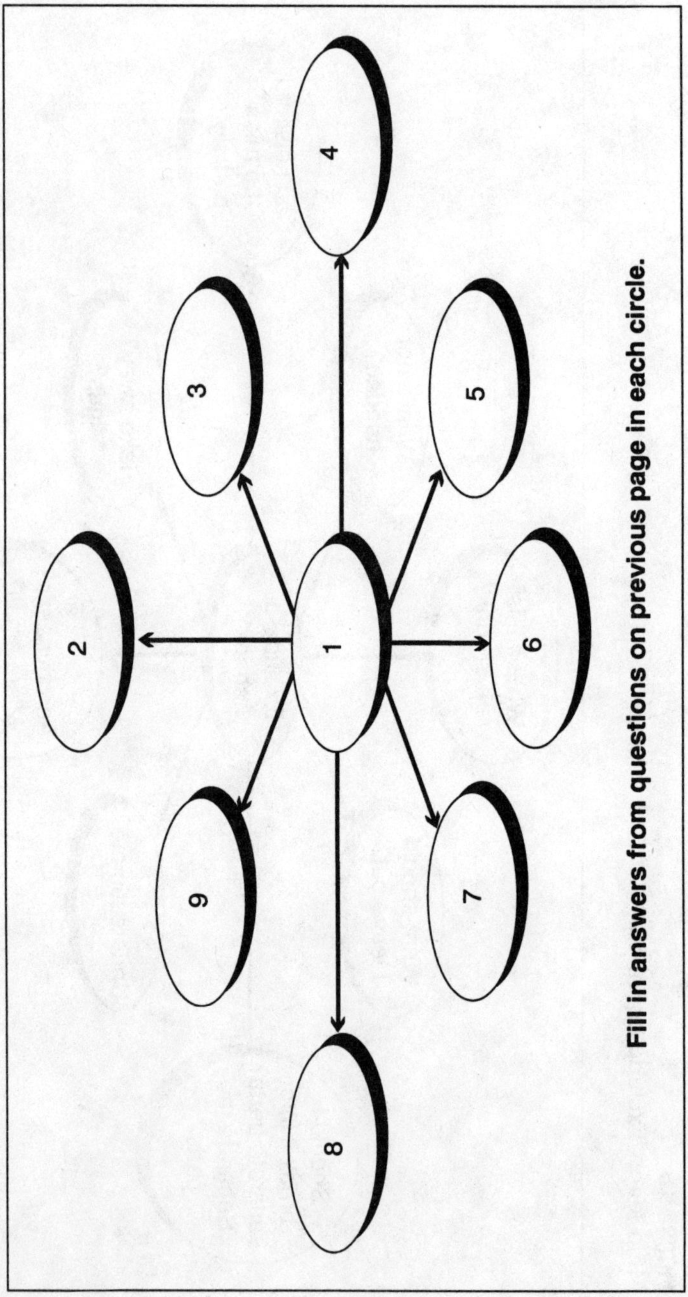

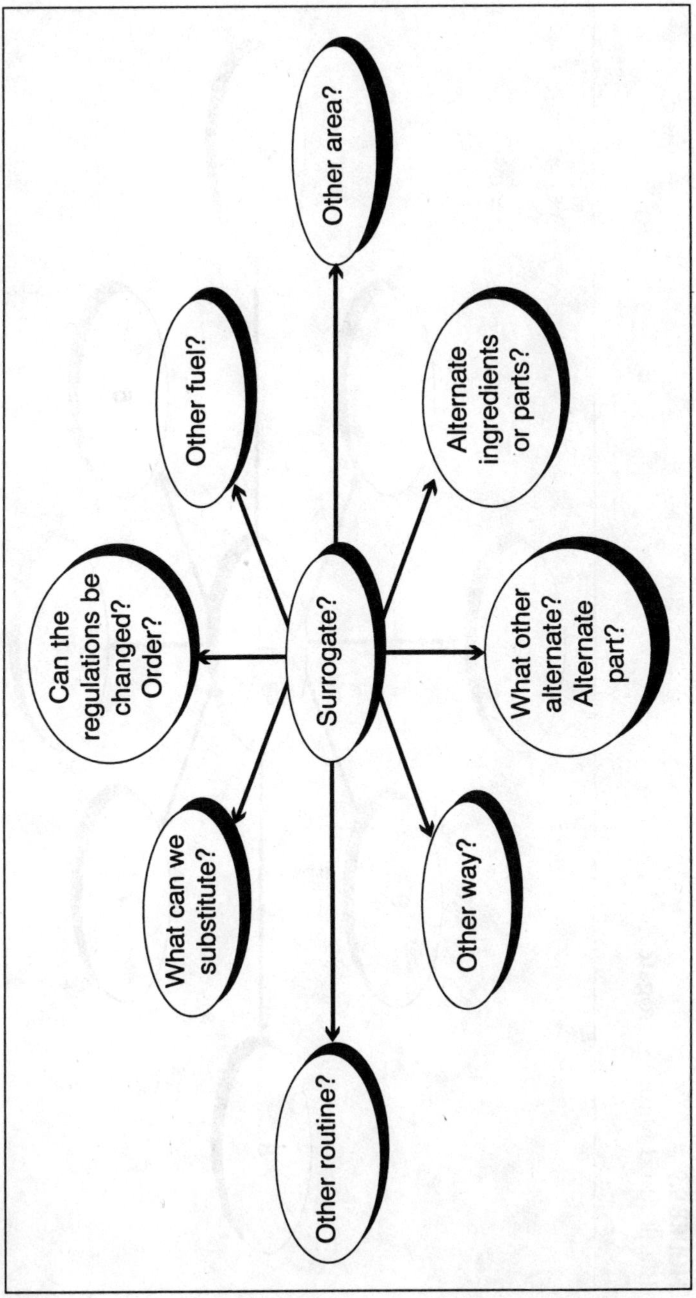

FIGURE 9.8
Mind Map: "Surrogate?"

FIGURE 9.9
Blank Mind Map: "Surrogate"

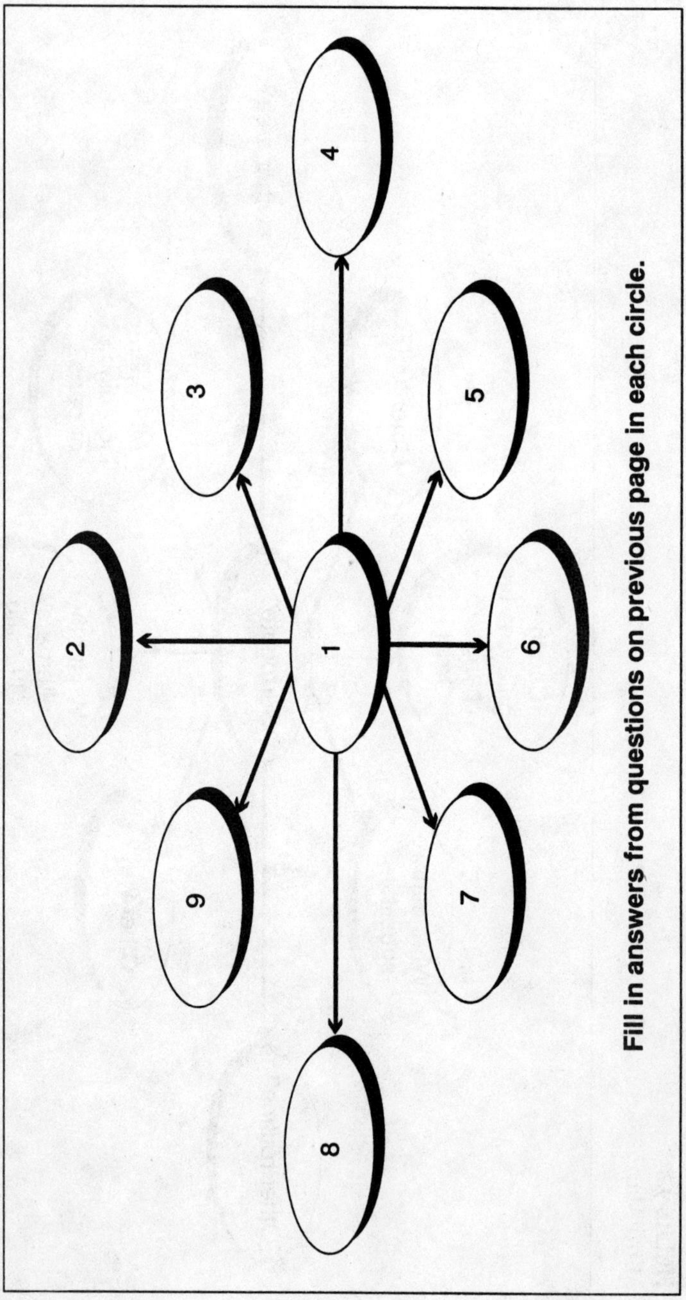

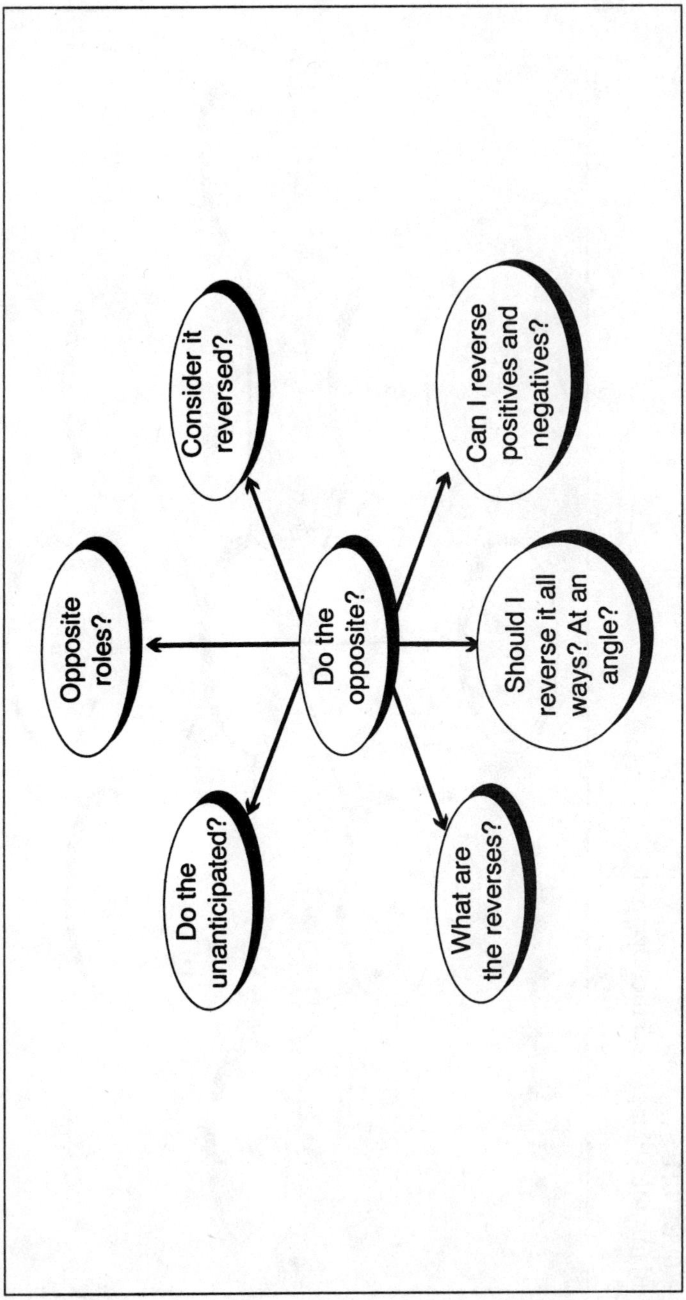

FIGURE 9.10
Mind Map: "Do the Opposite"

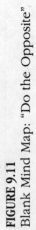

FIGURE 9.11
Blank Mind Map: "Do the Opposite"

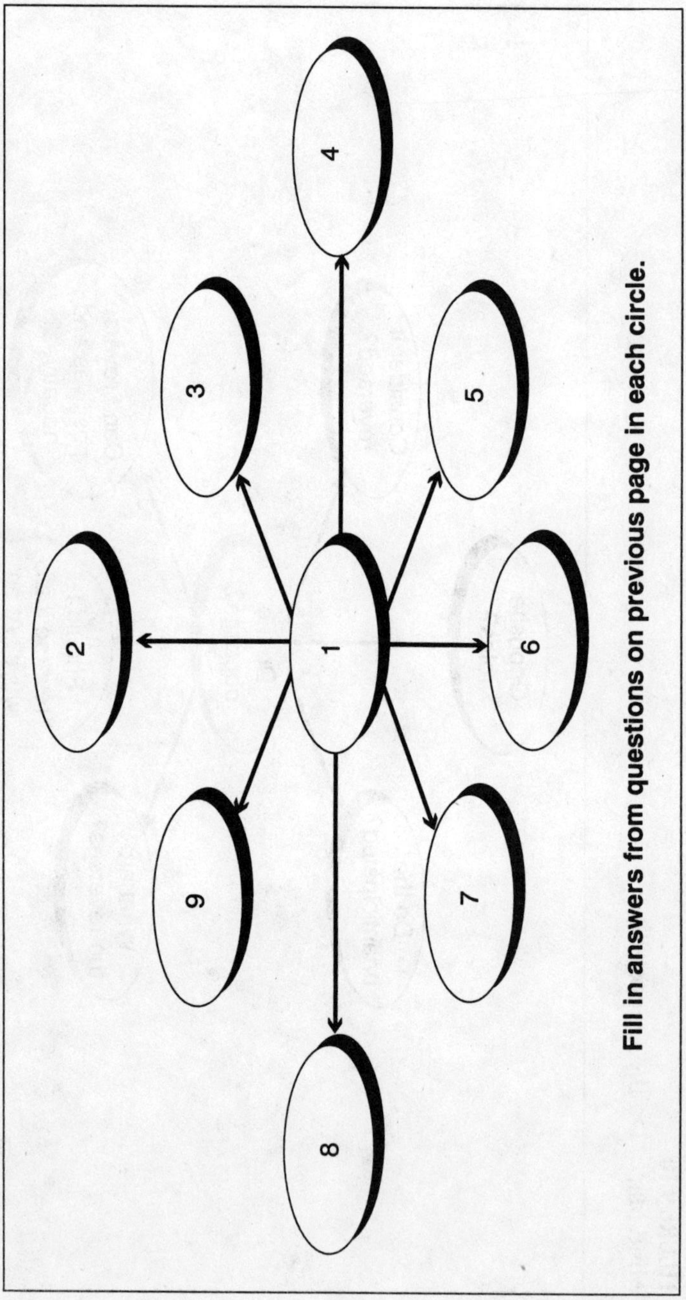

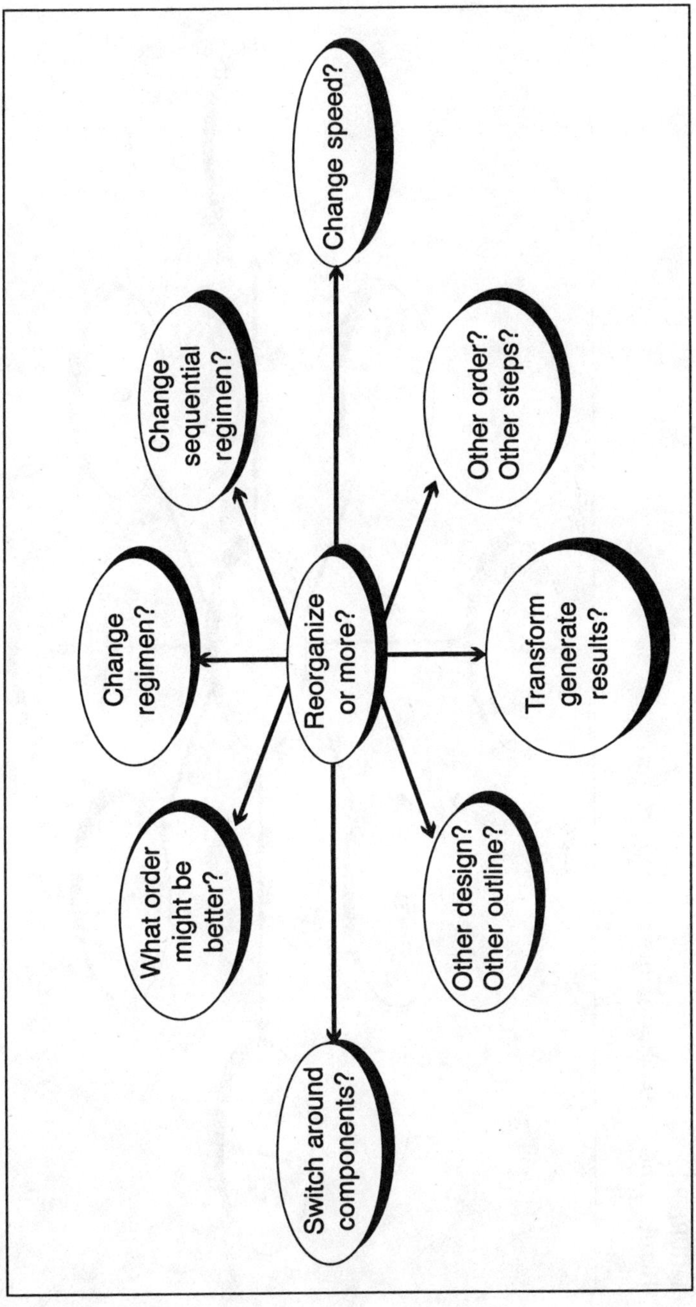

FIGURE 9.12
Mind Map: "Reorganize or More?"

FIGURE 9.13
Blank Mind Map: "Reorganize or More?"

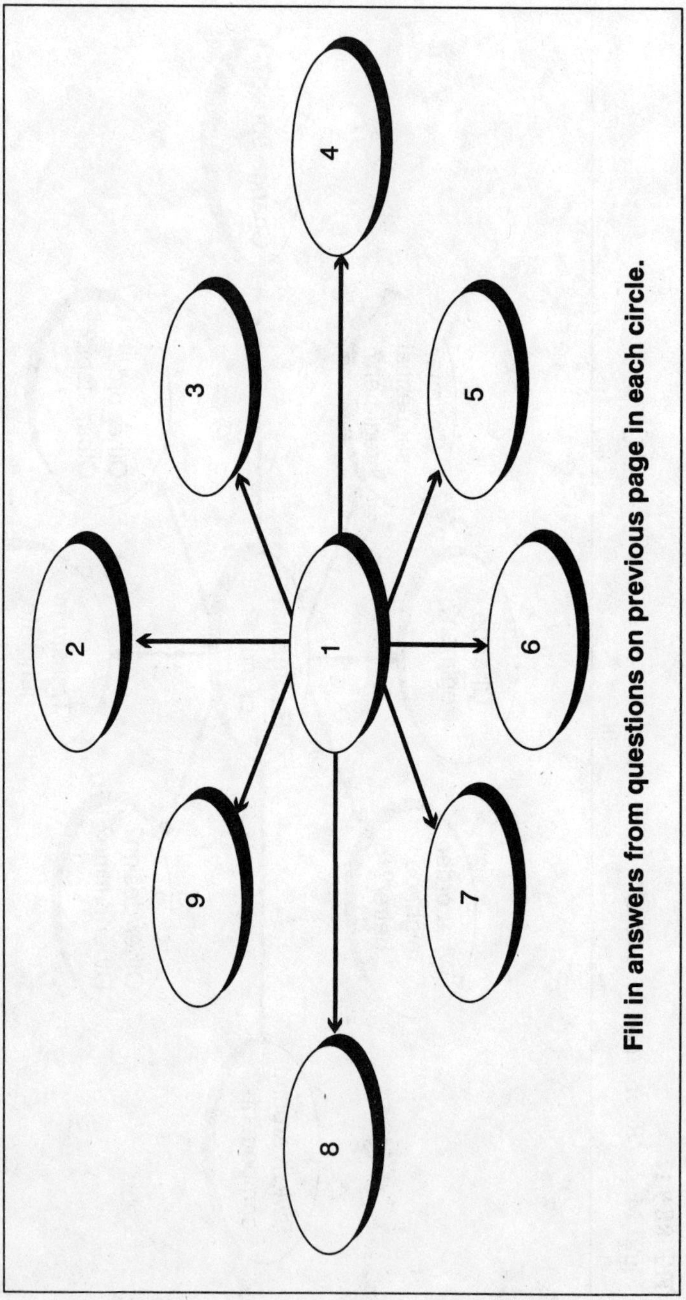

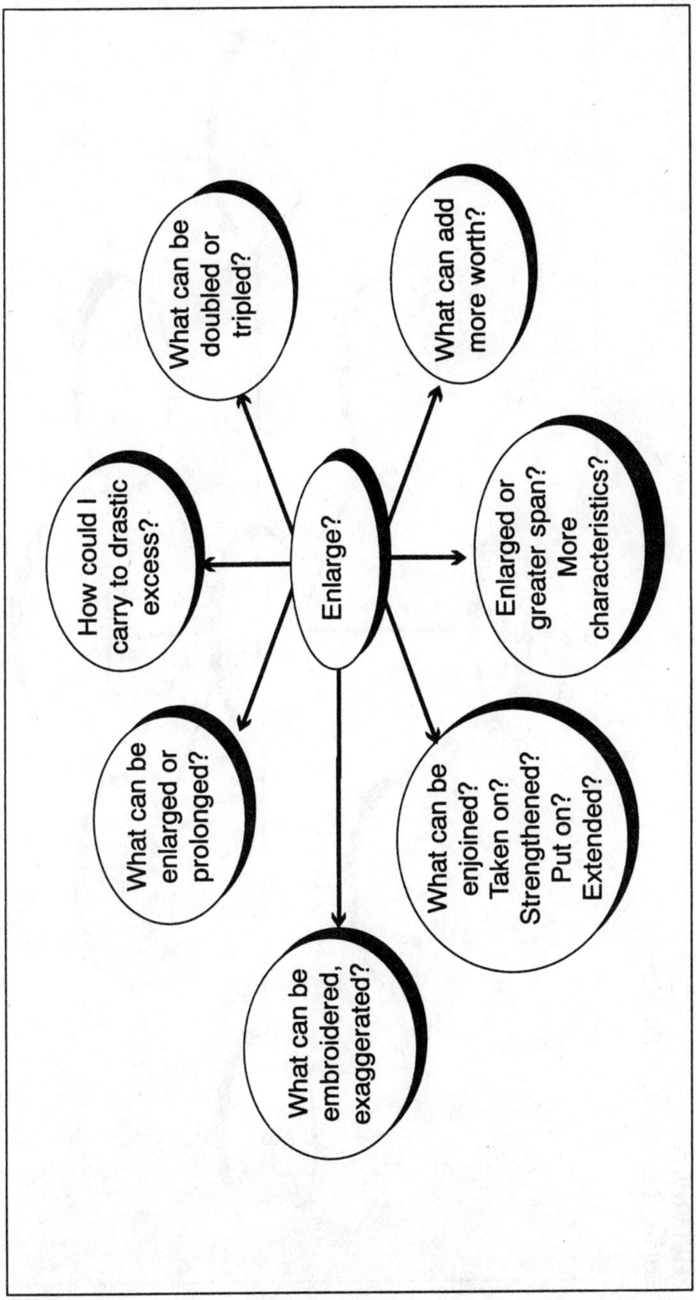

FIGURE 9.14
Mind Map: "Enlarge?"

FIGURE 9.15
Blank Mind Map: "Enlarge?"

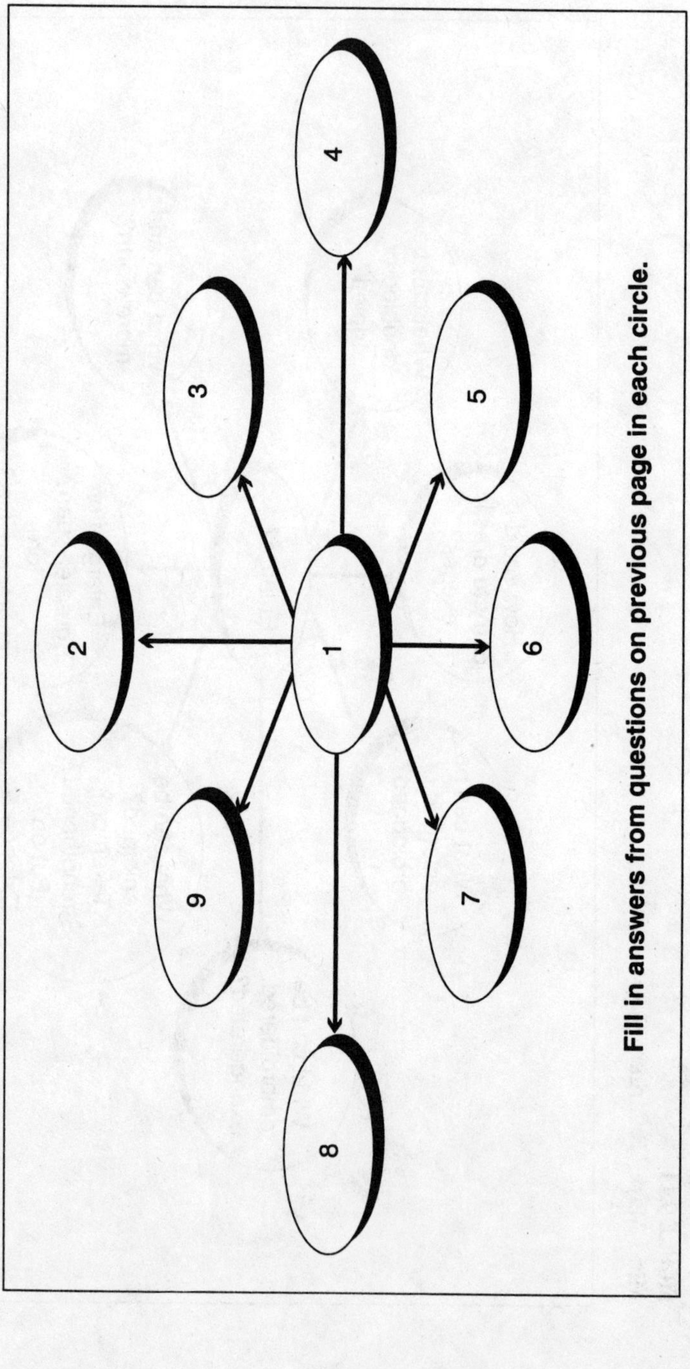

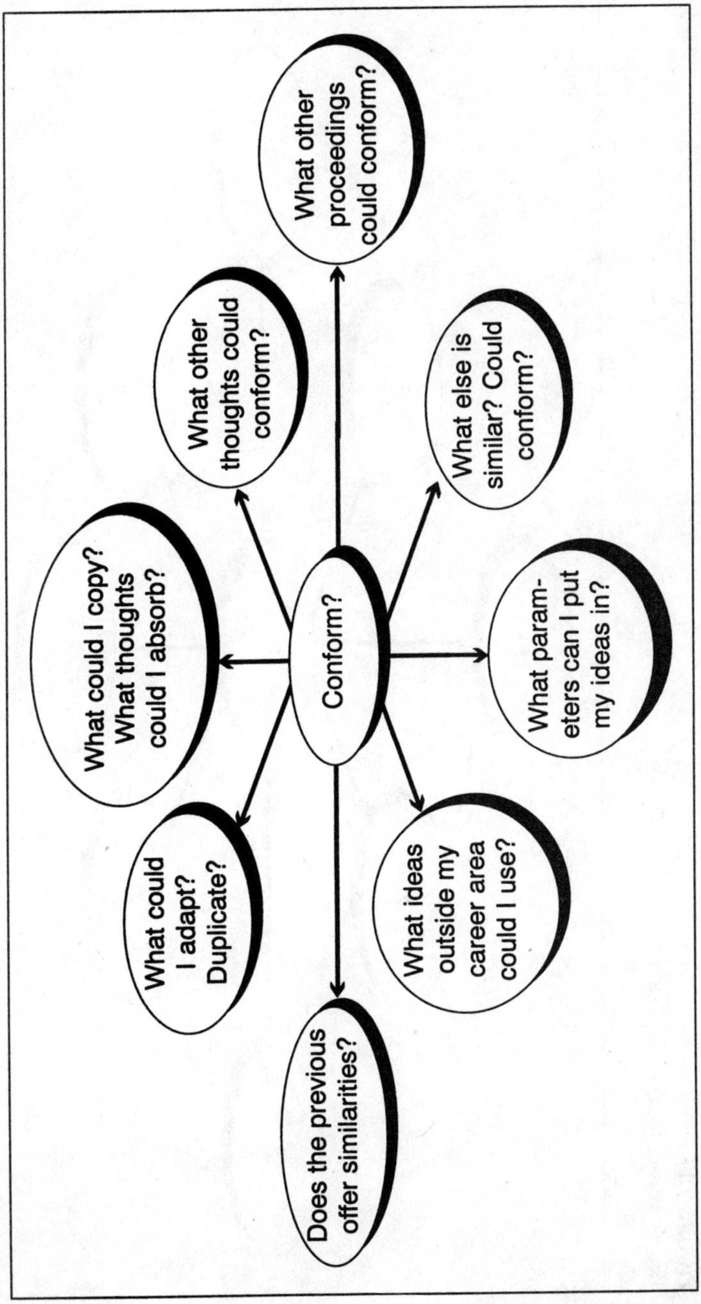

FIGURE 9.16
Mind Map: "Conform?"

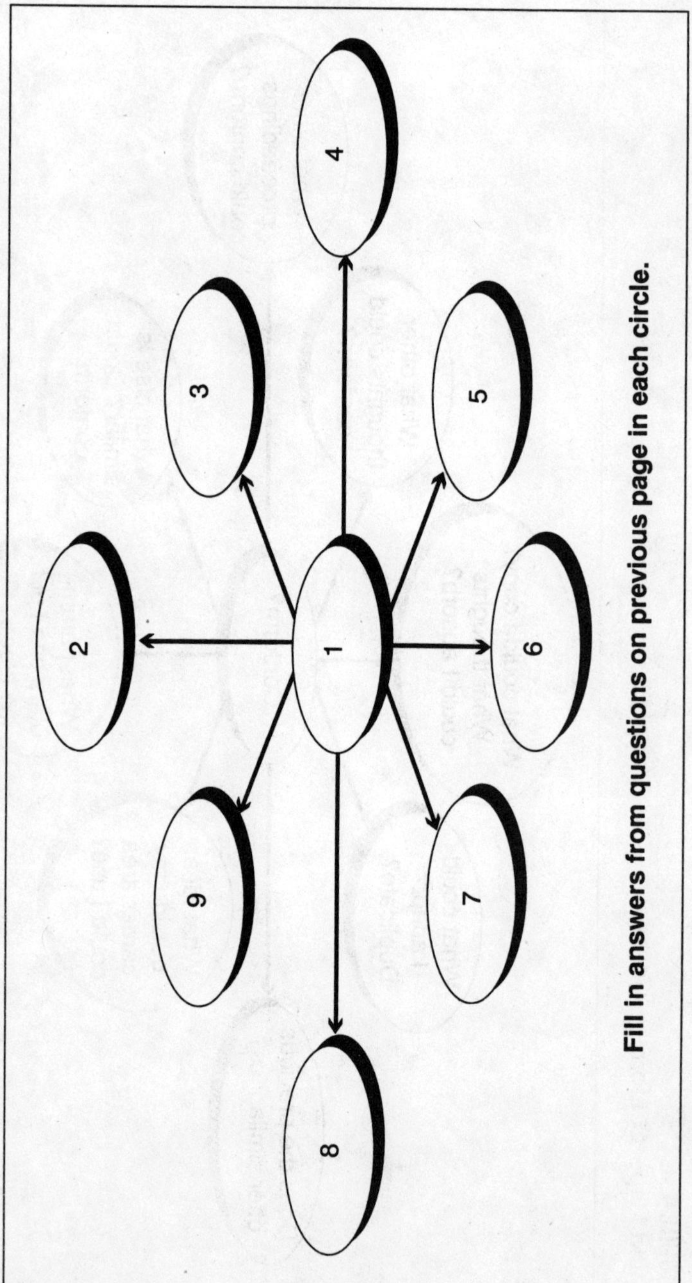

FIGURE 9.17
Blank Mind Map: "Conform?"

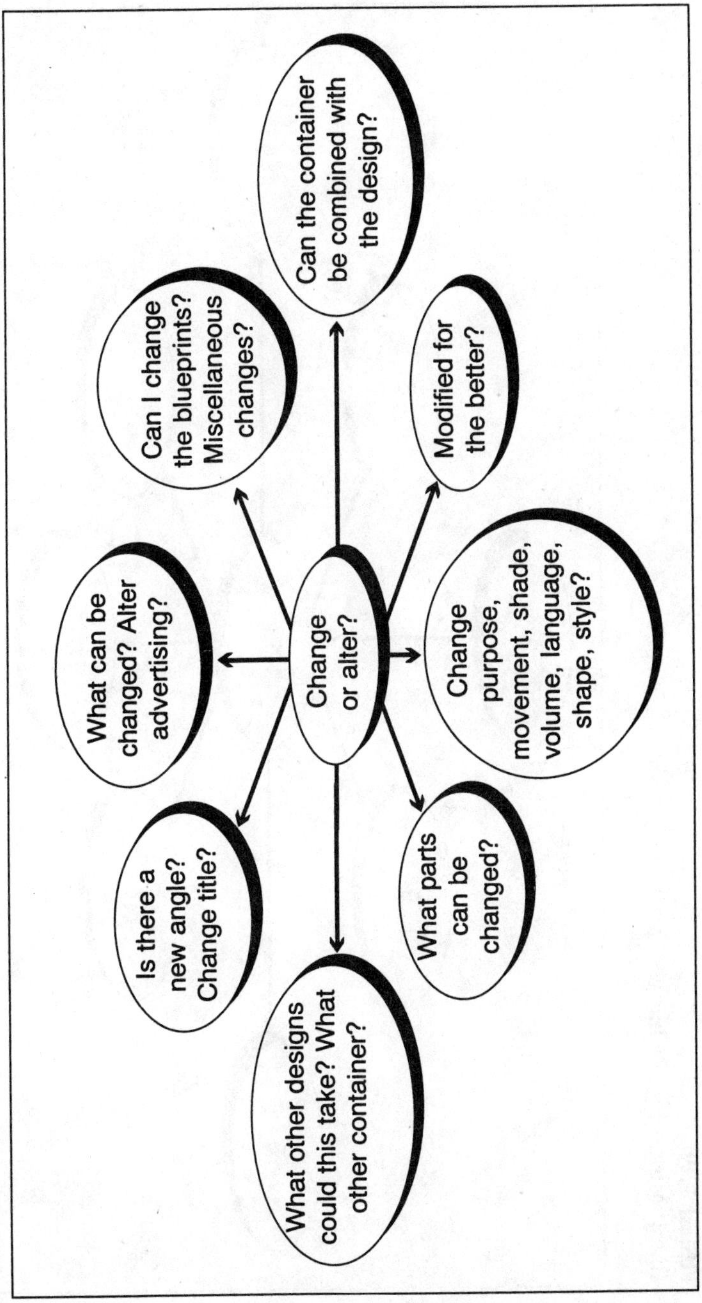

FIGURE 9.18
Mind Map: "Change or Alter?"

FIGURE 9.19
Blank Mind Map: “Change or Alter?”

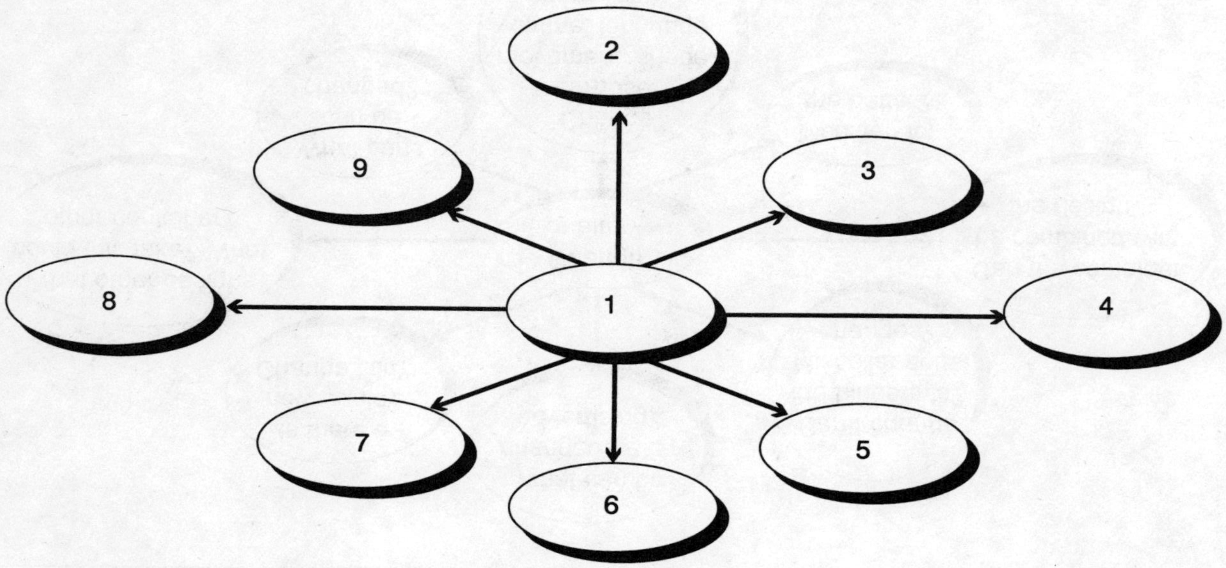

Fill in answers from questions on previous page in each circle.

FIGURE 9.20
Mind Map: "Other Applications"

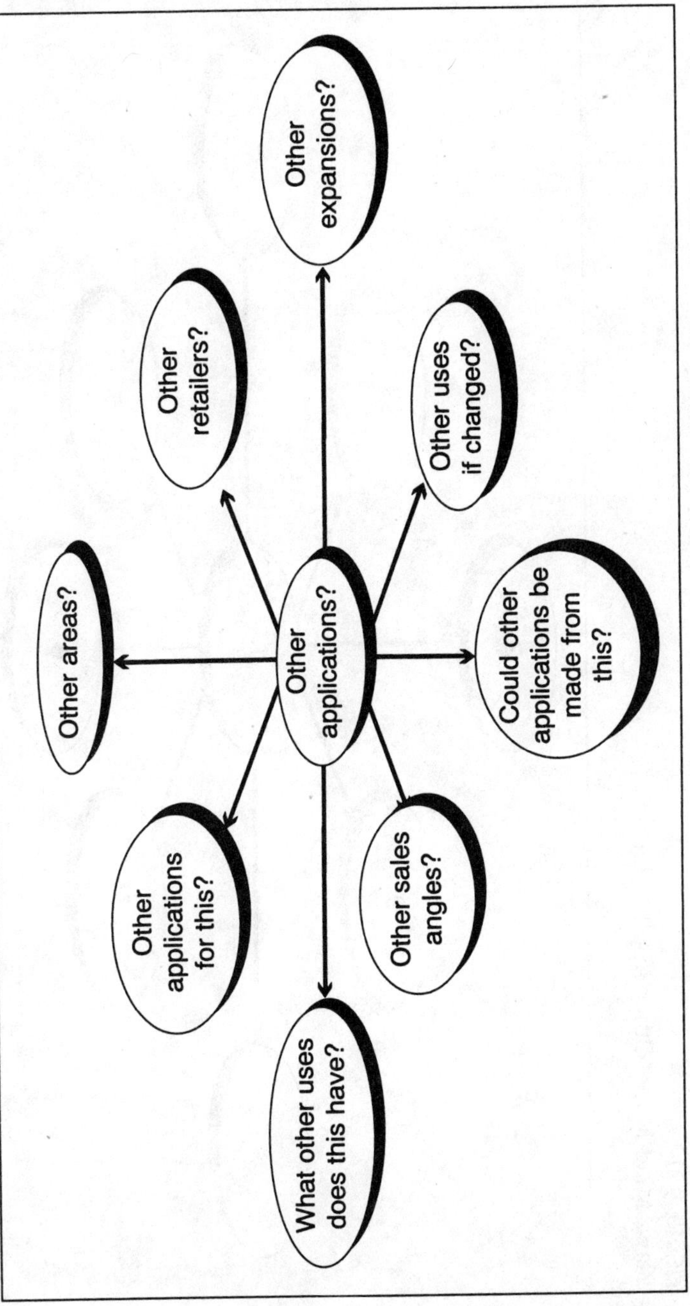

FIGURE 9.21
Blank Mind Map: "Other Applications?"

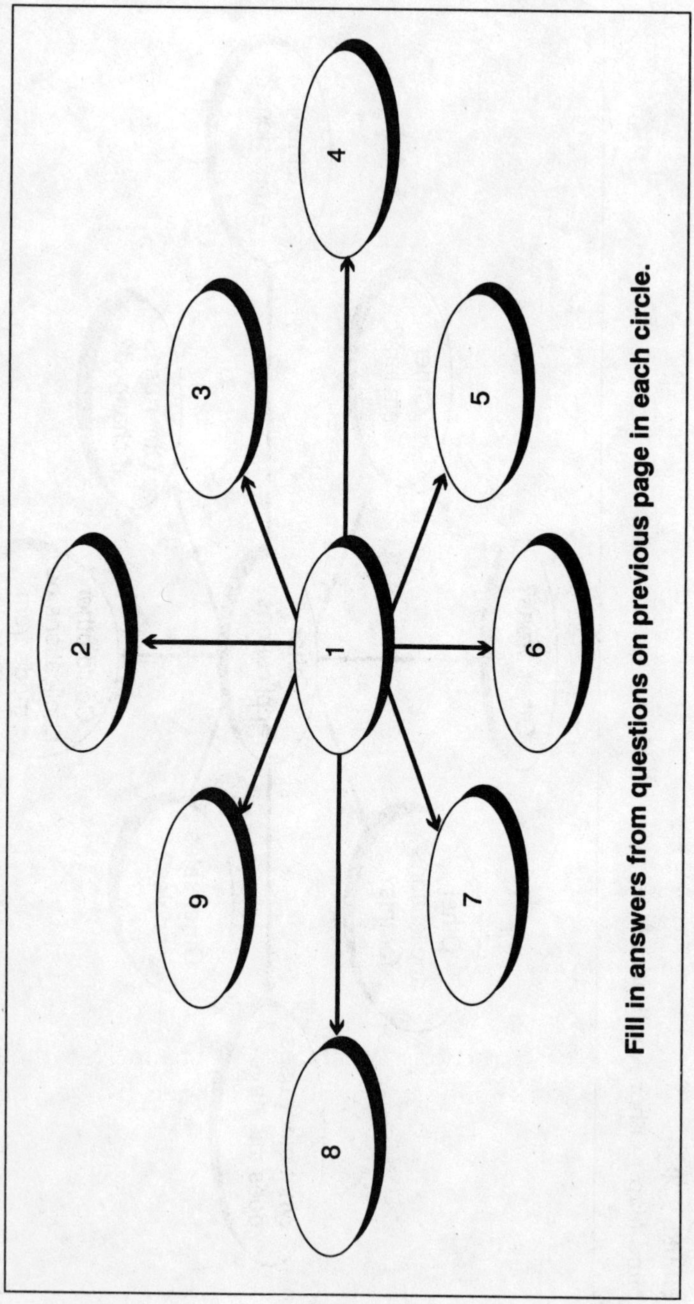

CHAPTER 10

Winning in the New Retail Revolution

My journey onto the information superhighway through home shopping has convinced me that a revolution is at work. Once the "big guys" routinely bullied us. Very talented inventors had to go abroad to get financing or let their idea die on the drafting table. However, the free market has prevailed. The options suddenly seem limitless. The "little guy" is no longer powerless. He has, by virtue of cable electronics, access to the same customer base as has any conglomerate.

There are almost as many ways to reach customers as there are people. Projections anticipate 500 channels, bringing $10 billion in sales on home shopping channels by the year 2000. We will be able to buy while flying at 40,000 feet through TV on airlines—all within just a very few years.

Entrepreneurs can realize their products with less expense and less risk. They can have personal control and build strong alliances with the forces that are shaping the marketplace—

home shopping channels. Insurmountable odds no longer impede great products, and they can reach the customer ever faster.

Let's review what we have covered in this book:

- The reason a one-person operation and a conglomerate are on a par is that communication now costs less.
- With very little time and money invested, you may now create a product and give it worldwide exposure.
- By profiting from our country's shift—from a manufacturing-based economy to a service-based economy to an information-based economy—those who are alert enough to both ride and create the trend are helping the free market flourish.
- Original information costs little to communicate. Information is *power.*

This power fuels your journey on the information superhighway. Where is it all leading? In my view, it is leading to the next step in our economic evolution—an idea-based economy.

Creativity is finally untrammeled. It is up to you to profit from it.

APPENDIX A

Contacts and Resources To Help You Succeed

Resources for More Information and Help

Federal Communications Commission (FCC)
1919 M Street, N.W.
Washington, DC 20554
Consumer Assistance and Small Business Division
Office of Congressional and Public Affairs: 202-632-7000
Library: 202-632-7100

The FCC covers cable television, broadcast stations and radio regulations. Their manual, the *Information Seekers Guide,* covers most communications topics.

Contact Sources for Home Shopping Channels

The Golf Channel
7580 Commerce Center
Orlando, FL 32819
407-363-4653
Fax: 407-345-4603

Home Shopping Network (HSN)
P.O. Box 9090
Clearwater, FL 34618-9090
813-573-5982
Fax: 813-573-3702

QVC Network, Inc.
1365 Enterprise
Westchester, PA 19380
610-701-1000
Fax: 610-701-1052

Value Vision
6740 Shady Oak Road
Minneapolis, MN 55344
612-947-5200
Fax: 612-831-0166

VIA TV
10001 Kingston Pike, Suite 55
Knoxville, TN 37922
615-671-1400
Fax: 615-671-1980

Video Catalogue Channel
7613 Blueberry Road
Powell, TN 37849
615-938-5101
Fax: 615-938-1210

Network Addresses and Phone Numbers

ABC
2040 Avenue of the Stars
Los Angeles, CA 90067
310-557-7777

CBS
7800 Beverly Blvd.
Los Angeles, CA 90036
213-460-3000

C-SPAN
400 N. Capitol St., N.W., Suite 650
Washington, DC 20001
202-737-3220

Discovery
7700 Wisconsin Avenue
Bethesada, MD 20814-3522
301-986-1999

Disney
3800 W. Alameda Blvd.
Burbank, CA 91505
818-569-7500

Encore
11766 Wilshire Blvd., Suite 710
Los Angeles, CA 90025
310-477-9922

ESPN
935 Middle Street
Bristol, CT 06010
203-585-2000

Family Channel
1000 Centerville Turnpike
Virginia Beach, VA 23463
804-523-7301

FOX
P.O. Box 9000
Beverly Hills, CA 90213
213-203-2026

HBO
1100 Avenue of the Americas
New York, NY 10036
212-512-1000

MTV/Nickelodeon
1775 Broadway
New York, NY 10019
212-713-6400

NBC
3000 W. Alameda Avenue
Burbank, CA 91523
818-840-4444

Showtime
1633 Broadway
New York, NY 10019
212-708-1600

TVS-TNT
1050 Techwood Drive N.W.
Atlanta, GA 30318
404-827-2664

USA
1230 Avenue of the Americas
New York, NY 10020
212-408-9100

APPENDIX B

Forms and Worksheets To Help You Succeed

FIGURE B.1
Goal-Setting Worksheet

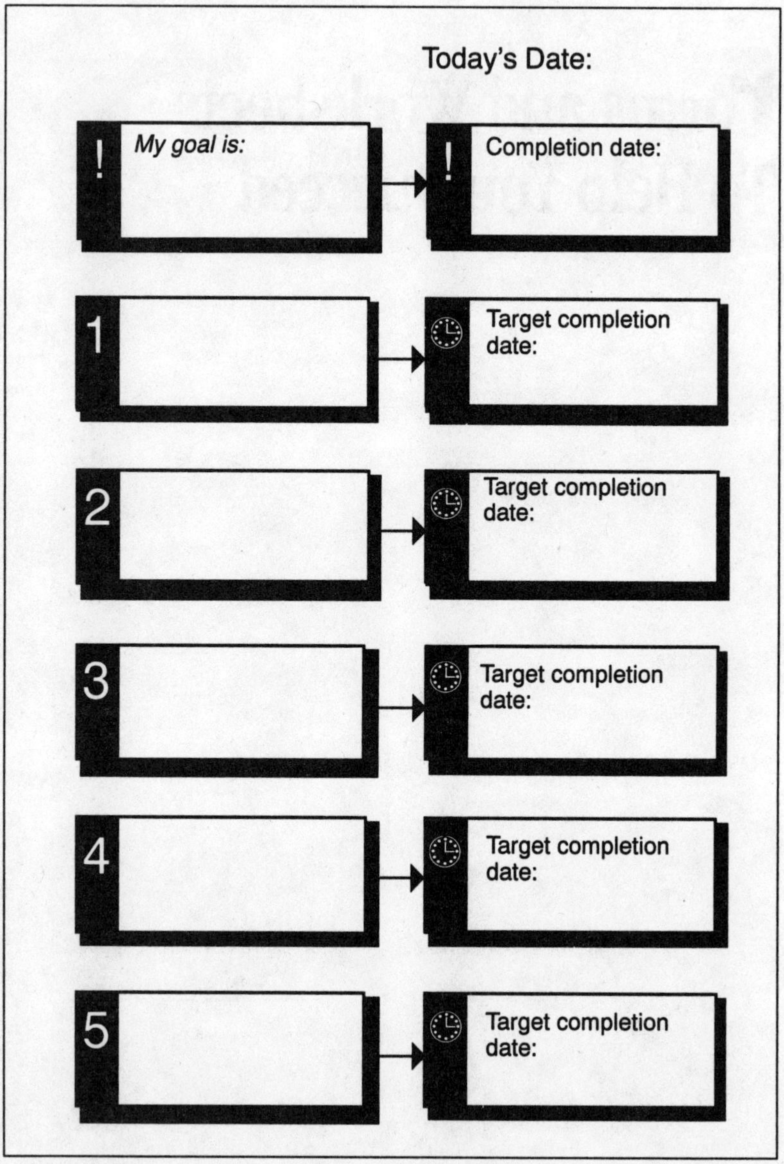

FIGURE B.2
Patent Goals

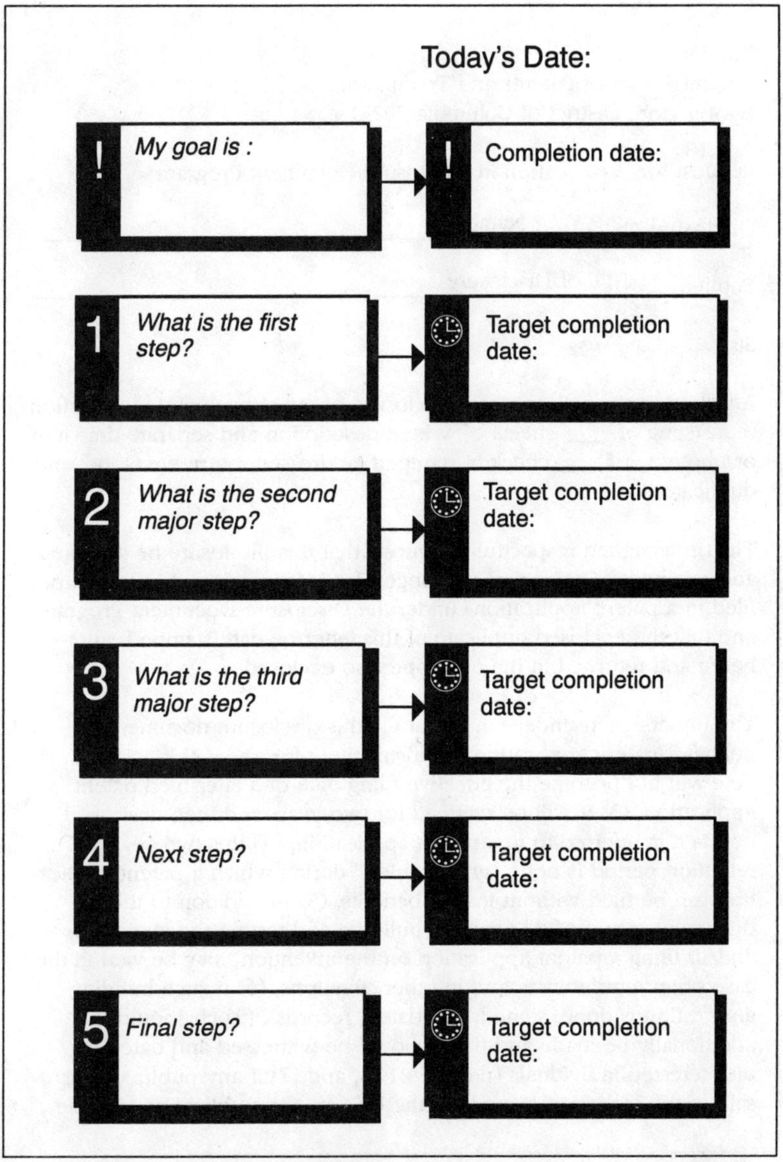

FIGURE B.3
Sample Disclosure Document

Box DD
Commissioner of Patents and Trademarks
Washington, District of Columbia 20231

Request for Participation in Disclosure Document Program

Disclosure of ___Your Name(s)___

Entitled: ___Title of Disclosure___

Sir:

Attached are two copies of a disclosure of my above-entitled invention (consisting of ____ sheets of written description and separate drawings or photos), a $____ check, a stamped, addressed return envelope, and duplicates.

The undersigned respectfully requests that this disclosure be accepted and retained for two years (or longer if it is later referred to in a paper filed in a patent application) under the Disclosure Document Program and that the enclosed duplicate of this letter be date stamped, numbered and returned in the envelope also enclosed.

The undersigned understands that (1) this disclosure document is neither a patent application nor a substitute for one, (2) its receipt date will not become the effective filing date of a later-filed patent application, (3) it will be retained for two years and then destroyed unless it is referred to in a patent application, (4) this two-year retention period is not a "grace period" during which a patent application can be filed without loss of benefits. (5) In addition to this document, proof of diligence in building and testing the invention, and/or filing a patent application on the invention, may be vital in the case of an interference, and in other situations, (6) if such building and testing is done, signed, and dated, records of such should additionally be made and these should be witnessed and dated by disinterested individuals (not the PTO), and (7) if any public use or sale of the invention is made in the U.S., or any publication is made

FIGURE B.3, *continued*
Sample Disclosure Document

anywhere, no valid patent can be granted on the invention unless a patent application is filed on it within one year of any such public use, sale or publication, regardless of the filing date of this Disclosure Document.

Very respectfully,

______________________	______________________
Signature of Inventor	Signature of Joint Inventor
______________________	______________________
c/o (Print Name)	Print Name
______________________	______________________
Address	Address
______________________	______________________

Note: Be sure you follow the first paragraph to perfection.

FIGURE B.4
Project Plan

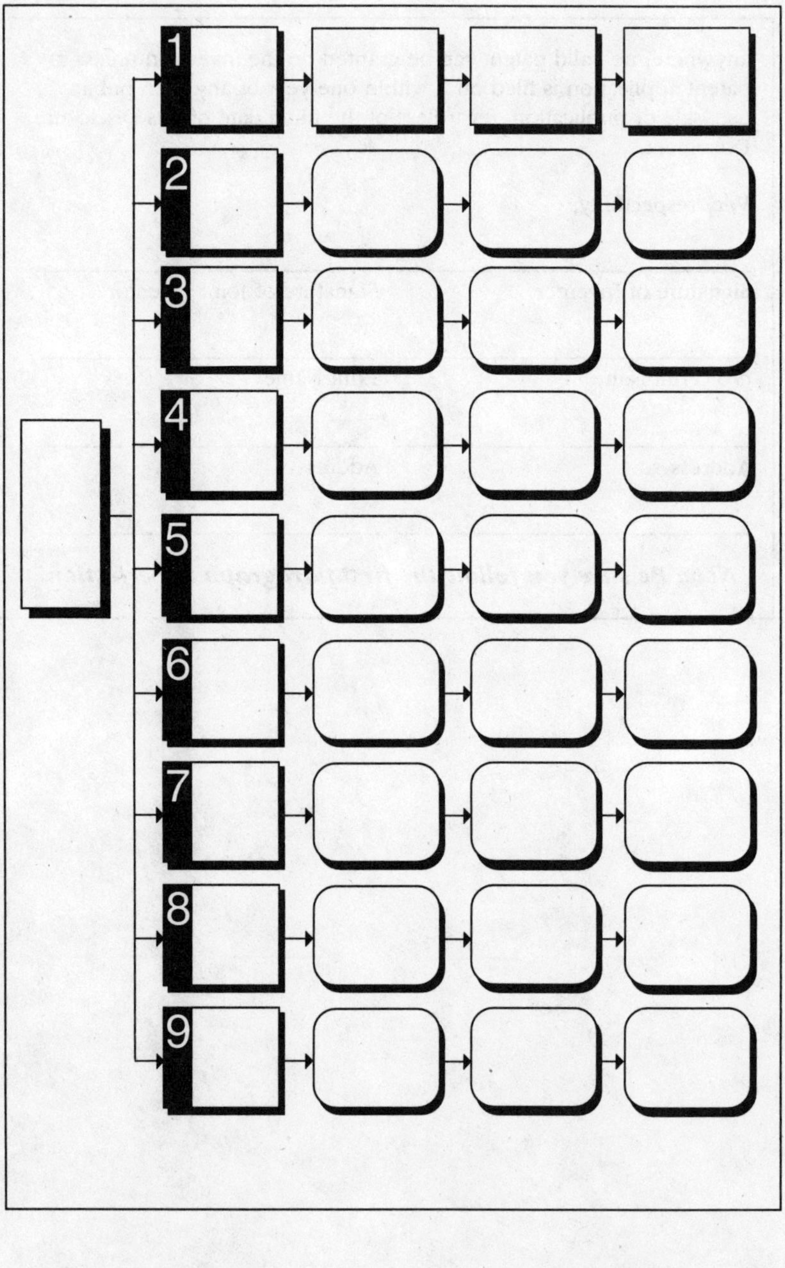

FIGURE B.5
Project Plan #2

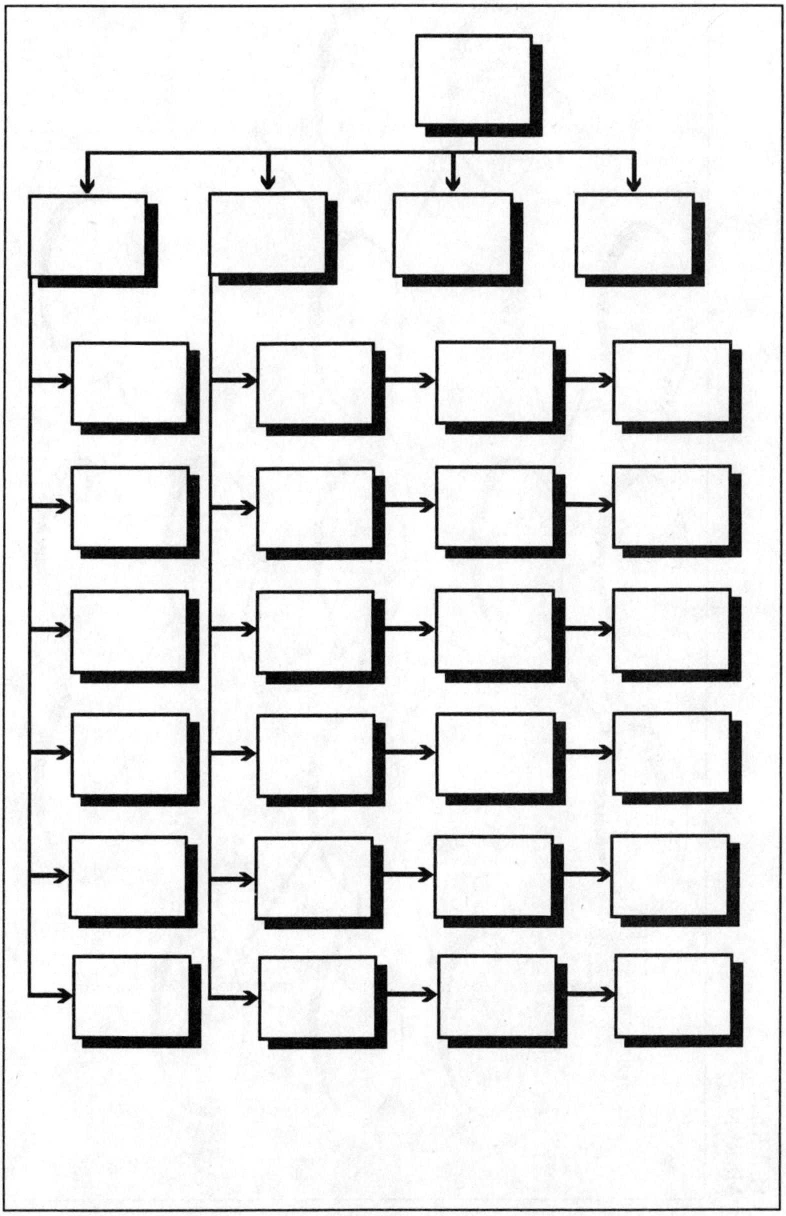

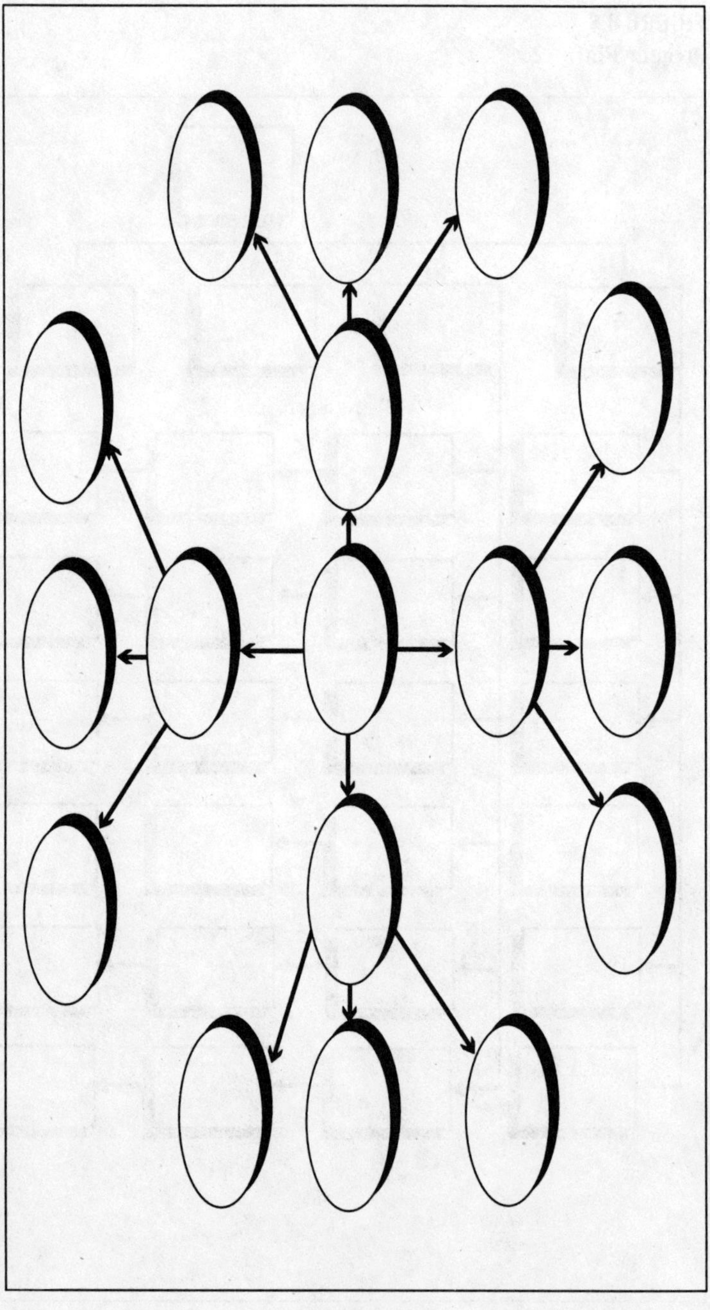

FIGURE B.6
Mind Map

Index